Find Me

as told to

Dan Baldwin

Find Me

a **FindMe**™ Publication

Copyright © 2012 by Dan Baldwin and Jerry "Kelly" Snyder

Printed in the United States of America

License Notes

* * * * *

Disclaimer

FIND ME: How a Unique Group of Psychics, Retired Law Enforcement Officers, and Canine Search and Rescue Volunteers from Around the World Have Banded Together to Find Missing People is not an approved instructional text for law enforcement, search and rescue activities, or for those who seek to assist in those operations This book is for entertainment purposes only, and nothing in it should be construed as encouragement to interfere in official police business or operations, or to intrude upon the privacy of individuals or families. The narrative and advice contained herein reflect solely the opinions, experiences and best knowledge of the authors, participants, and members of the Find Me organization, as told to Mr. Baldwin. Some names have been changed to protect the privacy of those involved.

* * * * *

Dedication

This book is dedicated to all the volunteer groups throughout the world that assist families and law enforcement agencies during times of crisis. These dedicated groups accept this responsibility solely for the purpose of helping people, with no expectation of reward or notoriety. In some cases these individuals put their own lives in harm's way but embrace the challenge. These same individuals do not consider themselves heroes, just loving and caring people doing something they believe in.

* * * * *

Acknowledgments

Find Me wishes to thank a very special group of people who have made enormous contributions to our efforts and to the success of this book.

Gary Cascio, of Late Nite Grafix, as Santa Fe-based graphic design firm, used his considerable skills to provide a powerful and moving cover design under serious deadline pressure.

AZ-STAR, Arizona Search, Track and Rescue, our sister group has climbed mountains, scrambled over desert boulders, and explored long-deserted mines with skill, courage and always good humor.

* * * * *

Testimonials

"During my thirty-five years of work in both the public and private sectors, I have made use of psychic resources on hundreds of investigations. Overall, my success in locating missing individuals has improved dramatically since first using a psychic resource in 1985."

~ Stephen C. Kopp, Retired Law Enforcement Officer and Private Investigator

"If you are interested in developing your psychic abilities, in helping others, and in serving a higher calling, then I would recommend *Find Me*."

~ Sonia Choquette, Best Selling Author of *Trust Your Vibes*

* * * * *

As told to Dan Baldwin

Credits

Cover photo by Dan Baldwin.

Formatting and cover design by Harvey Stanbrough.

* * * * *

FIND ME is a non-profit 501c3 corporation.

* * * * *

Find Me

How a Unique Group of Psychics, Retired Law Enforcement Officers, and Canine Search and Rescue Volunteers from Around the World Have Banded Together to Find Missing People.

With

Dan Baldwin, Dave Campbell, Stephen D. Earhart, Mary Surrena, Jeanette Healey RN, Sunny Dawn Johnston, Nancy Marlowe BA, Joanne Miller, Eileen Nelson, Loretta Greazzo, Chris Robinson, Amanda Achell, Kelly Snyder

as told to

Dan Baldwin

ISBN-13: 978-1475142952

ISBN-10: 1475142951

Find Me

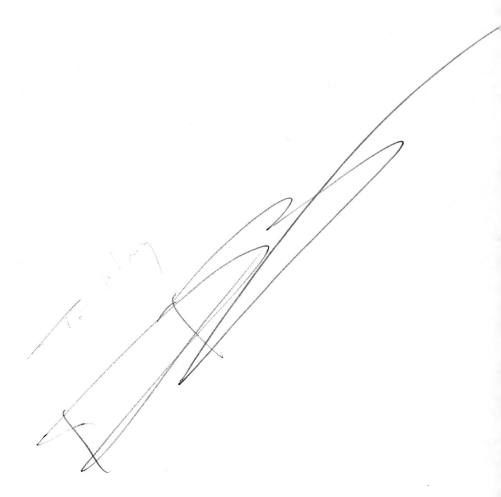

Table of Contents

Find Me

as told to

Dan Baldwin

Prologue

Act well at the moment, and you have performed a good action   for all eternity.
~ Johann Kaspar Lavater

A letter to the Find Me group:

I can't begin to tell you and the whole group what your service has meant to all of us that love Ed or to begin to know what it would have been like to not have had your group involved. I truly believe that without your group who knows the time frame in which he might have been found – if ever. After speaking with Christi (Arizona Search Track And Rescue) and Kelly (Find Me) I went from frustration and feeling hopeless to having comfort that a group having the capability and resources cared and would do everything you could to find him. And you did. What heroes you all are.
-Rhonda Younger

A Yavapai County, Arizona, deputy sheriff stopped to check out a truck parked on the side of I-17 at mile marker 310, about twenty-six miles south of Flagstaff. The vehicle was open and empty, with the keys still in the ignition. No one was to be seen in the area.

The time was 2:15 p.m., April 29, 2006.

The deputy didn't know that Ed Hatfield had recently come to Arizona from North Carolina to find work, or that he was severely depressed over a number of personal challenges. The deputy also was unaware that the truck's owner was walking up a nearby ridge overlooking Rattlesnake Canyon, and was no more than a quarter mile away. Ed was wearing his favorite cowboy hat. He carried a pack of cigarettes, a bottle of whiskey

1

and a loaded .38 pistol.

At the same time the deputy was checking the abandoned truck, Ed was calling friends, including Rhonda, his girlfriend of two years. Some days later, these North Carolina residents would realize that his unusually emotional calls were a series of goodbyes. Meanwhile, Ed continued walking up to the ridge. Although an avid hiker, he was wearing cowboy boots that made scrambling over the rocky hillside a struggle. When Rhonda was able to return his call, he was winded from the effort. He kept walking during their conversation.

In about twenty minutes, Ed reached a beautiful spot overlooking the canyon, out of sight and sound of the busy interstate. The spot offered a magnificent 360-degree view of a spectacular mountain forest. He climbed a tree and strapped himself, smoked a few cigarettes, drank some whiskey, and allowed the sun to deepen and darken the shadows before him.

No one heard the shot.

Days later, Kristi Smith of Arizona Search Track and Rescue (AZ STAR) received a call from Rhonda. Could they -- would they -- help find the missing man? Rhonda explained that the Yavapai County Sheriff's Department had said they needed more information before they could start an investigation, and that their "hands were tied." The department's Forest Patrol Section had told Rhonda that they didn't have a "point of entry," so their efforts were hampered as well. They had done a cursory search of the area, but came up empty.

Kristi wasted no time kicking things into high gear. She contacted Kelly Snyder of Find Me.

"Count on us. We're in!" replied Kelly, who immediately sent out an alert to the members of Find Me. E-mail is a prime communication tool for Find Me because, in addition to its Arizona contingent, it has members as far away as London, France, Australia and Italy.

Soon reports were coming in from Find Me members. Several contained virtually the same information: Ed was no longer alive. He had received a deadly wound. His body was southeast of where his truck had been left. His body was exposed to the elements. He would be found within a twenty-minute walk of the truck site.

Find Me and AZ STAR often partner on investigations and searches, and the mix is an amicable and effective one. Since the location of Ed's truck was known, the groups decided to conduct an on-the-spot search using Find Me's psychic information, psychics themselves, AZ STAR personnel, and cadaver and scent dogs. Kelly contacted the Yavapai County Sheriff's Department and Forest Patrol. Find Me and AZ-STAR are big on following proper protocol.

"This is how it's supposed to work," says Kelly, "Find Me's psychics working with a well-trained and disciplined search and rescue group, with the full cooperation of the police authority in charge of the case. All the elements came together."

Two searches were conducted: Wednesday, May 10th, and Sunday, May 14th. Kelly and fellow Find Me member Dan Baldwin were on hand to represent the group on both occasions.

The search area was marked in grids on topological maps to guide the search and rescue (SAR) teams, who also worked with radios and GPS monitors. Although, a significant amount of the primary search area was covered Wednesday, and although several of the dogs "showed interest," Ed wasn't found.

The group returned early Sunday morning to avoid the inevitable Arizona heat. Several of Ed's friends from Phoenix and North Carolina had been passing out missing-person fliers, and were on hand to "wait it out" at the command post. Provided with the psychic information and the appropriate search grids, the first group of canine teams set out to find Ed.

Within a few hours, Claudia Schmitz and Anita Sheelings, along with recently certified canine team member Jazz, (team #129) reported in. They had found cowboy-boot footprints, and Jazz was "on scent." They had the scent but, once again, Ed's body remained unfound.

Because of the rocky terrain, they decided to retrace some of their steps. Once again, Jazz "alerted," raising his head. Anita, the dog handler, and team support member Claudia followed the dog's "head up and on scent" lead. They looked up. That's when they saw Ed Hatfield's lifeless body, roughly twenty feet up in the tree, overlooking 360 degrees of the valley below.

Everyone's worst fears were true.

The team followed the appropriate protocols, and immediately sealed off the area to protect the potential crime scene. They simultaneously notified the command center and called for the remaining search teams to return to base. Kelly, Dan and Kristi climbed the ridge to help secure the scene. The Yavapai County Sheriff's office was immediately notified by Kelly, as were key members of Ed's circle of friends so they could make the necessary calls in North Carolina.

Sadly, Ed was found on Mother's Day.

Shortly, deputies from the sheriff's department and members of the Forest Patrol arrived at the scene to investigate and remove the body. After the appropriate interviews with investigators, Find Me and AZ STAR volunteers were officially released from the scene.

Why do people who could easily be playing golf, enjoying a relaxing day with friends and family and so on, hike around rattlesnake-infested desert and mountains to look for human "needles in a haystack?" Why would a bunch of psychics scattered around the world (most of whom have never met face-to-face) give up countless hours, days and weeks to find missing persons, knowing full well there's no reward or publicity to be gained from the case?

"This is what we are called to do," says Dan Baldwin.

Find Me's goal is to be called into action from the beginning of an investigation by local authorities. In Ed's case, it wouldn't have made a difference. But the resolution would have been quicker, and the anguish of not knowing minimized. The efforts of Find Me and AZ STAR are for the purest of reasons, to find missing people, help law enforcement, and bring closure to the families.

Kelly Snyder says, "We're all volunteers. We don't accept reward money. We don't get our picture in the local news. But when I get a letter or an e-mail thanking us for making a difference and caring from someone like Rhonda, well, that makes all the effort worthwhile."

"Please know you make a difference in people's lives," she wrote. "What heroes you all are!"

A spur-of-the-moment act based on a coincidence often leads to dramatic, and sometimes radical, life changes. Seemingly random occurrences and coincidental acts can bring about the most amazing results. Such are the curious set of circumstances that led to the formation of Find Me.

Of course, psychics won't be shy in telling you that there's no such thing as a coincidence. Paths cross. People meet. Groups form and lives are changed. But there's very little, if any, randomness involved. The universe often acts in mysterious ways, but rather than question those events, the people in Find Me accept the challenge and proceed with the purpose of "good action" in the hope of building and protecting a better world.

Introduction

From its inception, the aim of this book has been to acquaint the reader with a new and unique investigative technique that, coupled with experience and application, will lead to the successful completion of many investigations.

Reading this book will not make you an accomplished investigator. Investigating is not, after all, a science but an art whose techniques are far too numerous to be found in one publication. Investigative techniques such as interviewing and surveillance are acquired through trial and error, self critique, patience and practice.

The reader can, however, avoid many months, or sometimes years, of endless searches by incorporating psychics into his or her arsenal of investigative sources. It is the object of this book, then, to introduce the reader to an investigative source that has been successfully used by many investigators throughout the world.

While often chronicled in the print media and on television talk shows, this technique is not taught in recognized law-enforcement officer (LEO) schools or "three-letter agency" seminars.

Perhaps no other technological advancement has had such a far-reaching impact on the investigative community as the Internet. But psychics can perceive, through the eyes and ears of other people, occurrences in the past and future that will never be seen or heard on the Internet.

During my thirty-five years of work in both the public and private sectors, I have made use of psychic resources on hundreds of investigations. Overall, my success in locating missing individuals has improved dramatically since first using a psychic resource in 1985. While most of my experience has been in the location of missing people, I have used psychics on both civil and criminal investigations where there were few, if any, "logical" leads.

Quite often, the information provided by these resources has saved hundreds of hours of investigative time and pointed the investigators or authorities in the right direction. A good example of this is the location of evidence. How many times have you heard investigators say, "If we only could find the weapon!" Psychic resources are surprisingly helpful when searching for that "needle in a haystack."

Unfortunately, the acceptance of these resources in the law-enforcement community has been fractional. Many departments have policies that preclude the use of psychics, while others accept information, but provide little or no feedback to the resource. Having worked on both sides of the street, I can understand the legal and ethical issues involved. It is also quite evident to me, in looking back at numerous investigations, that the information provided by psychic resources was the turning point in successfully resolving many a case.

The basics of most investigations still require one to identify "who, what, why, where, when and how." Even the best investigator is occasionally stumped by one of these basics. My experience has been: When all else fails, use a psychic resource and see what develops.

Stephen C. Kopp

Retired Law Enforcement Officer and Private Investigator

Founding Find Me

with Kelly Snyder and Dan Baldwin

> *"You have to trust your inner knowing. If you have a clear mind and an open heart, you won't have to search for direction. Direction will come to you."*
> *~ Phil Jackson*

"Pure investigation and luck were not enough."

Kelly Snyder is a retired law enforcement officer with more than twenty-five years of experience, primarily with the Drug Enforcement Administration, U.S. Department of Justice.

After retirement, Kelly became very involved in working with young people. An availability of time, combined with a desire to contribute to the community and an interest in the health and well-being of children spurred him to join Big Brothers and Big Sisters. He also joined the National Center for Missing and Exploited Children (NCMEC), attended training sessions and the NCMEC academy.

While at the academy, he met a Mrs. Wetterling and a Mrs. Nick, mothers of children who had been abducted and were presumed dead. The women spoke of their traumatic experiences and how those experiences had affected their lives. For Kelly, those were defining moments.

"I knew then that I was meant to work finding missing children," he says.
Kelly began working in the field, and soon began to feel that there was more to be done.

"I realized that just pure investigation and luck were not enough. Most children abducted by a predator are dead within four hours. I knew that other tools, such as the Amber Alert system, needed to be employed to even the odds," he says.

Thoughts about alternative approaches eventually turned to alternative investigative tools.

"I'd had zero experience with psychics, intuitives, astrologers, mediums and the like, but I thought, 'Why not research this idea and see if their skills and gifts would be useful in locating a missing child?' My approach is to do what it takes and let nothing get in the way."

Events took time. But in a roundabout way, and within an amazingly short period, three unique paths crossed. A talented psychic, who was teaching a Tarot card class, on Friday 13th of all days, met a young man seeking help through hypnotherapy. During a conversation, he mentioned that his dad, Kelly, worked with NCMEC and was wondering about the possibility of organizing a group of psychics to find missing children.

Within a month, Kelly was attending one of the psychic's workshops. Mutual interest in finding missing people led to one of those "why don't we" moments. That's where the idea of Find Me began to become reality. Although this psychic has since left the group to pursue other avenues, her enthusiasm for the concept and her network of contacts in the psychic community gave Find Me a head start.

"Find missing children"

Dan Baldwin is a professional writer, often a "ghost writer" for other professionals. Some of his psychic friends get a real kick out of his business card, which includes the word "ghost." Dan has co-written or ghosted more than thirty books. He also is a certified clinical hypnotherapist, and he teaches a course called "The Practical Pendulum." (For more about Dan's story, see Chapter Eight.)

During one of his frequent late evening walks, Dan received a powerful psychic message.

"I heard a voice say, 'Find missing children!' It was almost a command," he says. The command was repeated a number of times during the next several months.

"Clearly I was being given a life mission...or going nuts."

Dan decided that the command was a legitimate mission. He answered the call and began searching for effective "tools of the trade." One day while discussing such matters with the owner of Well Spring Books in Mesa, Arizona, Dan noticed that one of the store's psychic readers was paying him some inordinate attention. She was continually flipping Tarot cards, and Dan finally realized, "She's flipping cards on me!"

Introductions were made. The reader said that she had started flipping cards because she recognized his interest in finding missing children. Her "knowing" had discovered a kindred spirit. It was no coincidence that they were both working on the same case, a young girl from Arizona missing without a trace. They began a working partnership on that and other cases that continues today.

This brings up an interesting point. Dan had never considered himself a psychic, certainly not a psychic detective. He'd never given a "reading" and had only recently begun a serious study of psychic techniques. The Tarot reader clearly saw something Dan hadn't yet realized.

You might be in the same position. We're all psychic to some degree and, chances are, most of us know a lot more people using psychic abilities than we realize. We don't need to showcase or brag about our abilities, but neither should we "hide our light under a basket." It's very likely that you have more kindred spirits (of the earthly sort) around you than you realize. Don't hesitate to speak up. You might be surprised to learn who'll respond, "me too!"

This paranormal phenomenon is considerably more common than popular thought would have us believe. Sometimes the people closest to us have abilities, but choose to hide them. There are many reasons. Some fear the paranormal. Others believe it's a manifestation of "the dark side," like the malevolent force in *Star Wars*. Still others don't understand, don't want to understand, or just chalk their experiences up to coincidence. And some choose to become psychic detectives, join groups such as Find Me, and do their best to serve their fellow humans.

One case the psychic and Dan worked that year provides an important lesson for intuitive investigators. A young girl had gone missing in far south Texas. As they attempted to find her, Dan used his pendulum and a process of elimination of locations to zero in on the girl's position. The psychic used her Tarot cards and worked with her spirit guides to get similar information.

As he was closing in, Dan asked an important question. "Is finding this girl in her best interest? Is this effort for the greatest good?" His pendulum began a strong swing toward the "no" position.

Dan backed out of the case and filed no more reports. The psychic's subsequent investigation led to the same conclusion. Although they had found the girl at a specific location, both investigators agreed that sometimes it's in the "missing" person's best interest to remain missing.

"Is taking on this case for the highest good? That's a basic question and one that should be asked before you begin any investigative work," says Dan.

If you haven't guessed by now, this psychic was the same person working with Kelly to found what would become Find Me. Dan was asked to join, and he became the third member of the group.

Find Me now consists of some twenty individuals in the United States, Britain, Italy, Canada and Australia. They are a diverse group, coming from different backgrounds and with different skills and gifts. Many members have contributed to this book. They've all given time, effort, heart and soul to finding missing people, solving crimes and even working to track down criminals and prevent crimes.

Every member doesn't work on every case. Personal schedules, personal interests, involvement in other cases, and, for some, a need to be "called" to a case often dictates who can work a given situation. Every member is actively involved in some case at any given time, and many work multiple cases.

Does psychic detecting actually work?

"Hell, yes it does, just not as often as we hope it would," says Kelly. Of course, that's the rationale behind Find Me. The more clues that can be developed, the greater likelihood of solving the crime.

"The main focus of any group like ours is that everyone has to be doing this for reasons that are pure, and not with the thought of charging for our services or reaping any form of financial benefit for our efforts," says Kelly.

One of the founding tenets was that Find Me would seek neither reward money nor notoriety. There are legitimate expenses for the group, with travel and food forming the majority of out-of-pocket expenditures, but so far it has not been that bad, according to Kelly.

Somewhere down the road, he hopes that Find Me can obtain non-profit status to open the door for financial contributions. This also will allow members to travel and, most importantly, upgrade equipment – a desperate need. The successes of Find Me will further dictate these necessities in the future. Word has spread, however. Initially, the group volunteered its services for compelling cases. That still occurs, but more and more authorities, search and rescue teams, families and individuals are seeking out the services of Find Me.

As with any organization, evolution takes place. The original focus was limited to seeking clues to help locate missing children.

"However, when a family member who has a missing brother, sister, father, mother, relative or friend asks for help, we decided it didn't make sense to turn anyone away," Kelly explains.

One area the group has so far avoided is looking for runaway children. This might change in the future, but no runaway cases have been worked so far. The potential of finding and helping return a child to a potentially abusive, even life-threatening, environment is a major concern.

Canine search and rescue resources have been included in Find Me full time. This seemed to be the final but most necessary addition to the group.

The building of Find Me is not complete by any means. The organization continues evolving. New people with additional skills, abilities and experiences continue renewing the capabilities, spirit and commitment of this dedicated group of volunteers.

As this book was being written, Find Me was actively working cases from the desert Southwest to the bustling Northeast, and even overseas. Local police and sheriff's departments, search and rescue teams, missing-person organizations and individuals and families are now calling the group for help in a variety of cases. Without publicity or public relations efforts, the word on Find Me has gotten out. Members are active, aggressive and dedicated to their work. They are committed to the "good action" that is required to make our world a better place.

As Napoleon Bonaparte said, "There are but two powers in the world, the sword and the mind. In the long run, the sword is always beaten by the mind."

Medium

with Loretta Greazzo and Jeanette Healey, RN
> *At the heart of each of us, whatever our imperfections, there exists a silent pulse of perfect rhythm, a complex of wave forms and resonances, which is absolutely individual and unique, and yet which connects us to everything in the universe.*
> *~ George Leonard*

Rarely does a psychic get a complete picture of an event. Rather, bits and pieces related to the incident "come through."

For example, when working on a case for Find Me, one member might receive visual images. Another might hear sounds or words. Another might pick up impressions from handling a physical object, or might dream about an element of the event. Still another might not receive anything at all. Generally, a given psychic detective will pick up only a piece or a couple of pieces of the puzzle at hand.

The thinking behind Find Me is basic – the more pieces of a puzzle you can assemble, the more likely you are to form a complete picture and solve the mystery.

A member of Find Me had received a considerable amount of information about the kidnapping of a young girl. The information was so voluminous and so specific that he approached a detective working on the case. The psychic was worried about the reaction he'd get from the police department.

Would they "blow him off"? Would they laugh? Would they consider him a suspect because of his "inside" information?
Much to his surprise and relief, the detective was open and respectful while he conducted a tape-recorded interview. At the close of the session, he offered his thanks, adding, "You know, last year my biggest case was solved by a psychic."

Of course, the detective said that after turning off the recorder!
Most people would be surprised to learn how much and how often law-enforcement authorities across the nation and around the world work with psychics. You probably wouldn't be surprised at how reluctant they are to admit it. And who can blame them?

"And how did you solve the murder, detective."

"Well, there's this lady who looks at pretty pictures on colorful Tarot cards, you see."

"Oh, really?"

Or:

"How did you solve the murder, sheriff?"

"Well, there's this guy who swings a rock on a string over a map, and he tells me where to look."

"Say what?!"

Or:

"How'd you find the little girl, officer?"

"Well, there are these folks who talk to dead people and…uh…never mind."

Make no mistake about it: Crimes have been solved with the direct aid of psychics. Missing persons have been found, "bad guys" have been brought to justice, and mischief has been averted with the advice, counsel and direct intervention of psychics. Right now, men and women of all ages, all faiths, all races, and all points of view are using an amazing variety of skills to do their bit to improve the lot of humankind.

They are especially effective when joined together in a group like Find Me, where all their disciplines and skills can be combined again and again to solve a single problem.

The team solution

As an example, Dan Baldwin and a number of psychics were attempting to locate a missing person who had disappeared from a small town in the central Arizona desert. Foul play was suspected, and the man easily could have been taken to any part of the state.

One psychic consulted her Tarot cards and another asked her guides. Dan employed a pendulum technique known as "map dowsing." Others, using such techniques as remote viewing, provided additional input. Their work became focused on the area in and around a specific desert "wash" (dried riverbed) several miles from the town, but neither could get an exact location where the man (or, more likely, his remains) could be located.

They finally pinpointed an area roughly five miles long, following the wash, and about half a mile to either side. If they were to verify this, only one course of action was available.

Dan, an avid desert hiker, laced up his boots, strapped on his water bottles, put on his cowboy hat, and headed into the desert. He began walking a crisscross pattern from east to west, always following the wash. Fortunately, the terrain was fairly flat. Still, there were undulating hills, rock outcroppings, ditches, areas of dense undergrowth, and cactus patches. That meant a lot of walking back and forth, up, down, in and out, and even some jogging when encountering the occasional wandering rattlesnake.

One psychic believed that the man's body would be found in or near a well. Dan noticed a number of wells marked on his topological maps and, weekend by weekend, he crisscrossed his way toward them. Local police, working with cadaver dogs, beat him to the punch, however. The man's head was found next to the wash and near a well, about a mile from where Dan's last search grid had taken him.

"Of course, I wish we had been the ones to find the man, but the fact that we were in the right area and moving toward the right spot is all the validation of our work that I need," says Dan.

As you continue through this book, you'll learn how psychic detectives work, about their talents and abilities, about how you can develop your own innate psychic abilities, and how you can form an organization to help do your bit, too.

Ordinary folks, extraordinary gifts

How does one become a psychic detective? The stories of Loretta Greazzo and Jeanette Healey will provide key answers to that question.

Loretta says, "We all have the gift and, like any conventional skill, anyone can learn how to open the doors to developing their own intuitive, clairvoyant and medium abilities."

Loretta has known this since childhood, when she could sense people behind her, people who "were not there" – in other words, ghosts. She also showed strong intuitive abilities at an early age. These abilities, of course, were the cause of frustration, confusion, and perhaps a little fear among her friends. The mysterious events also caused a considerable amount of personal concern. The early years of a psychic's life are difficult enough without the added burden of having paranormal abilities before you know how to put them to proper use.

"Had I known then what I know now, I would have felt comfort and not frightened," she says.

Do we all really have psychic ability?

Of course, and this gets a unanimous nod from all the psychics in Find Me. How many times have you been thinking of someone you haven't seen for quite some time, and then *voila*, he or she calls you on the phone, sends you an e-mail, or runs into you unexpectedly? How many times has the phone rung, with you instantly knowing who's there before you even pick it up?

Is that coincidence? Some would have you believe so. Psychics would say there are no coincidences. It's intuition, plain and simple, an ability everyone has. Since it's an ability, it's something that can be enhanced and put to good use.

Jeanette, who says she's sometimes been an "unwilling passenger" on her psychic journey, began experiencing the paranormal at age five. She became very confused because she could plainly see things other people couldn't.

Jeanette and her older brother spent all their childhood summers with their grandparents, who ran the New Inn Pub in the historic town of Dover on the southeast coast of England. This now lovely attraction is documented as one of the most infamous local hangouts for smugglers. It had tunnels running beneath, connecting it with two other pubs in Dover. Thus, they were known collectively as the "Three Ones."

The New Inn Pub also had a longstanding reputation for being haunted, and Jeanette experienced a number of psychic events when visiting, including an uneasy feeling, the sense of being watched, and "cold spots."

One day while playing upstairs, she looked up to see a young boy about her age staring at her. He wore black, shiny patent-leather shoes with silver buckles. His hair was blond and done up in ringlets. She'd never seen him before. Jeanette said, "Hello, who are you?" The boy didn't answer. She looked away for a second, and when she looked back he was gone, as if he'd just disappeared. Later on, she told the adults, including her mentor, Nan, what she'd seen.

"She has seen our little Georgie," said Nan.

Many years earlier, a child named Georgie had fallen down the flight of stairs near the upstairs bedrooms and had broken his neck. He'd been making appearances since that tragic accident, and his occurrence was a familiar event to intuitive folks visiting the pub. Some found the encounters disturbing. Others, such as Nan, accepted these appearances as part of the natural, if paranormal, order of the universe.

Nan helped Jeanette understand that her abilities were a gift, something not to be feared but to be celebrated and used for good. Eventually that advice led to Jeanette's work as a psychic detective, and brought with it the hard realization that you don't always get the hoped-for outcome.

Her first murder case involved a newborn baby found in a lake. Despite months of investigation by the police and news media, the case had stalled. Jeanette stepped in and volunteered her services. Her contact was an open-minded detective happy to receive any help he could get, even if that help came from "out there."

The information Jeanette provided made little sense. But, as a psychic detective, she knew that her job was to provide information and not to worry about the analysis and interpretation of that information. The material she provided included descriptions of the baby, articles to be found with the baby, and even the name of a girl related to the case.

The detective stared at the name and said, "You won't believe this, but she is next on my list of interviews this afternoon."

Jeanette was receiving important and verifiable information that might lead to the arrest and conviction of the culprit. The data she provided were so accurate that the detective asked her to visit the scene of the crime.

Upon arriving, the detective said, "All right, show me where the body was found." Despite the accuracy of the data Jeanette had already provided, he was still testing her and her abilities.

Jeanette gets "funny sensations" when walking near specific areas where such events have happened. These sensations came to her twice that day, once on each side of the small lake. The detective told her that the first place she pointed out was exactly where the baby's body had been found. The other spot was where authorities believed the baby had been dumped into the lake.

Jeanette then told him about psychometry, the ability to receive vibrations and images by holding physical objects related to the crime. They agreed that, since Jeanette would be handling physical evidence and her DNA would end up on it, she had to sign a paper stating that she had handled the evidence. Even in psychic detecting, proper protocols, procedures and paperwork must be observed.

Jeanette shared her impressions with a psychic artist, who was able to "tune in" to the images she was getting. Together they came up with a detailed drawing of a girl about fifteen years old who was the mother of the baby found in the lake. The girl, they felt, was still alive. And that was pretty much the end of the story.

The case remained unsolved despite all the information Jeanette had shared. Two years later, another detective arrived at her door. He carried a photograph of a young woman who had recently visited the grave of the baby from the lake. She was the "spitting image" of the young woman Jeanette and the psychic artist drawn. Unfortunately, the young woman disappeared, and the case is still on the unsolved list.

Jeanette still hopes for resolution, but is satisfied that she has done all she could do.

"The mother will turn up again, maybe tomorrow and maybe in twenty years. But the information my guide, Jack, gave me is down on record and, for now, that's enough."

A fair question

If psychic detectives are getting all these clues, why don't they just get the full picture all at once and solve the case immediately? Jeanette has some interesting comments on this most obvious of questions.

"We're only human."

Person-to-person and group-to-group communication is difficult enough as it is. You need only look at today's headlines for verification. Three people can see the same automobile accident and still file entirely different reports with the authorities. Imagine the difficulties encountered in attempting communication with a world of spirits.

"Information can be spot-on about one person, but with another, it could be slightly off regarding dates or other personal information."

Regardless of our line of work or our abilities in that work, we all have our "off" days. We all experience times when we're just not performing at 100 percent. Psychics are no different.

"Some days, certain things seem as clear as crystal, and another day you can be working through a fog," she says.

There's another factor rarely considered by the skeptics.

Jeanette says, "Remember that the spirit who is communicating with you may not have been a very good communicator when alive, and would probably be the same in the spirit world. After all, we're supposed to have the same personality after we cross over."

She believes in the "simpler is better" philosophy. Spirit communication isn't as difficult or complex as a lot of people seem to want to believe. Simple doesn't mean easy.

"It can be very frustrating to receive only a certain amount of the story," Jeanette explains. Of course, that's also part of a much larger picture. Why?

"Well, if we know it all now, there's nothing to look forward to when we pass over. I can't wait for the next installment and the excitement of finding out more."

She makes one last comment on the question. "There is corruption and incompetence in every walk of life."

That includes law enforcement. Sometimes, valuable information is given to professional people and it is still not believed, not used, misunderstood or in some cases misused.

"As psychic detectives, we have to do our best and then hand over the information in good faith."

Loretta's technique

Pray In. This is an essential step, Loretta emphasizes.

Always ask Whomever or Whatever you offer your prayers to for guidance. If you believe in Jehovah, Jesus, the Holy Spirit, Allah, Buddha, Gaia, the Goddess, the universe or the great unknown, pray in. If you don't have any religious faith, address the power of your subconscious mind to provide the guidance and wisdom you need.

It's important that you begin with a positive attitude, she says.

"Protect yourself. Again, pray for or ask your subconscious for protection during your psychic-detecting sessions. Visualize yourself surrounded by a globe of the purest white light that deflects any negativity coming your way. Whatever image works best for you is what is appropriate for you. Just remember to always step into your 'psychic armor' before you step into a psychic session."

She also urges meditation.

"Psychic detecting requires a quiet and focused mind, something that's a lot easier to seek than it is to find. After all, we're all busy, and our minds are a jumble of challenges at work, chores at the house, problems with friends and family, unexpected opportunities, and the mind-numbing clashes and clutter encountered in modern life."

As a psychic detective, you have to leave all that behind so you can concentrate on the job at hand. A life could depend upon it.

"Meditation is an easy and proven means of achieving a quiet and focused mind. Try this. Make sure you're in a quiet location where you won't be disturbed for at least ten minutes. If you've never meditated before, you'll be amazed at how quickly you become relaxed and how easily you can begin to focus and quiet a busy mind."

Here are a few exercises to get you started.

Set aside quiet time in an environment in which you won't be disturbed. Eventually, you'll be meditating for twenty to thirty minutes before a psychic-detecting session. Of course, if you want to meditate for other reasons, including just plain old relaxation, you can meditate for much longer periods. For our purposes, however, meditation is just the first step in the psychic process.

Be sure to wear loose and comfortable clothing. Pick a comfortable chair or couch where you can sit up straight with both your feet on the floor. Some people prefer to lie down, but be careful if you adopt this pose. You can easily become so relaxed you'll fall asleep and defeat the purpose of your meditation.

Place your hands on your legs or at your side with palms facing upward to keep the flow of energy open. Close your eyes and slowly take in some deep breaths through your nose and slowly exhale from your mouth. Repeat the process three or four times, then breathe normally, paying attention to your breathing without trying to alter it.

Become aware of every part of your body. From top to bottom or bottom to top, start feeling every part of your body sink into relaxation. Random thoughts will probably intrude and begin racing through your mind, but you have to maintain focus. A good way to stop these thoughts and clear your mind is to mentally keep repeating a peaceful word such as "relax" or "quiet" or "peace."

You can always go with the ancient standby word "om." Try it. It's hard to think of something else when you are focused on a single word or thought.

Playing soft music also helps, and you also can burn some mild incense or a scented candle. There's nothing ceremonial or magical about music and incense. They're just tools to cut down on some of the outside sensory input that can intrude and disrupt your meditation.

Now, relax and lose yourself in the process. Pay attention to any pictures that pop up in your mind's eye. We often get flashes of pictures in our mind during our conscious hours, but they're gone in seconds because our conscious mind is so busy that we don't pay attention. When you get an image, try to hold it and get as much detail as you can.

Do you see people? Are they tall or short? Male or female? What are they wearing? Are they dressed in clothing from this era or from another time? Don't be shy about addressing these ethereal folk. Ask them if they have a message to give.

Your image may be a scenic picture. Do you recognize the area? What are the surroundings? Is it winter or summer? Can you smell anything? Your image could just be a symbol. What kind of symbol? What color? What shape? How big is it? Is there just one? When you are finished getting as much detail as you can, tell yourself you are going to open your eyes now and feel better than you did before beginning the session.

If you don't see pictures but get certain feelings, remember what you're feeling and what sensations it gives you. Psychic information can come through all your senses. Did you smell anything? Did you hear anything? Did you taste or feel anything? Were there any emotions? All sensory inputs are valid, and all can help put more pieces into the puzzle you're building.

If you don't get anything, that's okay. Even the most skilled psychics have their "dry" moments. Professional writers often run into a "writer's block" that can derail their efforts for days, weeks or even months. Psychics can face the same kind of challenge. With the practice of meditation, you eventually will improve. Don't panic or fret. Don't try to rush it, and don't set yourself up for a fall with unrealistic expectations. As with any skill, the more you practice, the better you'll become. The information will begin to flow faster, easier and with greater clarity. If you did see or feel anything, write it down. Keep a journal of your experiences to help "connect the dots" of any case you may be working on, and to help monitor your progress.

After your first week, Loretta advises another approach. Enter your meditative state, but instead of losing yourself in nothingness, white light, or the sensation of total peace, try to visualize something enjoyable, such as your favorite flower, a walk on the beach, looking at the stars, and so on. Can you sense how the flower feels or smells? Can you see the detail of the flower, the stem, or the leaves? Can you see the waves rolling, feel the sand under your feet, or smell the ocean? Can you see the Milky Way or your favorite constellation?

Try to keep that vision long enough to get a feeling of it. This type of exercise will help you be aware of visions that cross your mind and help you hold them longer when they arrive during your conscious hours.

After a few weeks of practicing on your own, you can work with a friend by setting up a time when each of you will not be disturbed. Go into your meditative state and see if you can pick up on what your friend is doing at that very moment. Are you getting a picture in your mind of what he or she is doing, or are you getting a feeling or sense of it? Call your friend when you're done and see if the information you got was accurate.

Getting help from 'The Other Side'

Many psychic detectives receive messages from deceased family members, friends, total strangers, and even victims of crimes. The psychics who use this technique will tell you that the process is based in reality. They actually do make contact with individuals and groups who are deceased. Some skeptics will contend that the psychic is merely contacting his or her own subconscious.

Setting the paranormal aspects aside and thinking strictly in terms of finding missing people, does it really matter where the psychic input is coming from? Provided the information is accurate and can help solve the crime, who cares about the source?

Of course, psychic detectives, and anyone with a curious mind, do care. More than a technique for solving crimes, contact with the deceased raises fundamental questions. Direct contact answers more than a few.

Can we really receive information from what's commonly known as "the other side"? Rather than simply tell you something as fact, the members of Find Me encourage you to explore this area for yourself and to make up your own mind. If you approach the matter seriously, consistently, with respect and using proper methodology, you will get your answers.

Here's an experiment to get you started.

Sit in the middle of a completely dark room, as close to the darkness of a deep cavern as you can get. If total darkness is impossible, tie a bandana loosely over your eyes to help blot out intruding light. Pay attention to your emotions and senses. Notice what comes through. Do you feel physical sensations? Are emotions bubbling up? Do you get any images?

Don't forget to journal each session. Periodically review your notes to see if any new sensations show up. Journaling is also an excellent way to measure how far you have progressed from your first sessions. Be sure to date your entries.

Loretta says, "Here's how to use this basic technique to explore making contact with the other side. Relax. Pray in. Surround yourself with the divine white light of protection. Ask Archangel Michael, the angel of protection, or whomever you feel comfortable praying to, to protect you during this process and to only let through those who have love, truth and goodness in their hearts. This is very important. Just as there are good and positive forces in the universe who wish only the best for us and our efforts, there are very negative forces which have their own agendas. Our health and well-being and successful research aren't on that agenda. Psychic protection is an essential element of psychic detecting."

Go into your meditative state and ask your higher self or spirit guides, "What messages need to come through for me or anyone else for the highest and best good of all involved?"

"If you're trying to connect with a loved one or trying to help find a missing person, you can keep repeating his or her name. Give it time, don't rush it, and pay attention to all your senses. Do you feel someone, see someone in your mind's eye or do you just know someone is there? Maybe you hear someone either audibly or from within your mind, as if the thoughts were your own. If you make a connection, but don't know who has made contact, ask. Ask what message he, she or they have to give you. Allow yourself time to receive the information. Try to remember as much of the message as possible. When done, offer a sincere 'thank you' and then slowly come out of your meditative state, open your eyes and write down what you have received in your journal."

Your higher awareness and gut feelings will tell you if these messages come from love and truth, Loretta states.

"Never pass along a message to someone if you don't feel comfortable with the message or if it just doesn't feel right. Instinctively you will know what and what not to do. The more you use this technique, the more you improve your ability, the more you will learn to trust this instinct."

Don't get discouraged if at first you don't make contact with the other side, she says. Continue to practice and trust your instinct. You may only get a sense or feeling of knowing who they are, what they look like and what their message is. You may only see symbols, and you may or may not know what they mean.

"Symbols represent different meanings to different people, and each person must interpret the meaning according to his or her own personal life and experiences. You can find any number of dream-interpretation books and, as far as they go, they are okay. But symbols are very personal. A snake, a lion, a great height, the ocean, a tornado or whatever may strike terror in the heart of one person and bring joy or peace or wisdom to another. Again, trust your own intuition over any book. Don't question, judge or try to rationalize the information that comes through. By all means, keep your ego out of the process. There's just no room for ego when exploring your psychic awareness. Check it at the door before you walk in!"

Other awareness techniques

You can practice ways of expanding your psychic awareness in your everyday routine. While driving, see if you can pick up on which cars in front of you will change lanes or make a turn. In line at the grocery store, see if you can get a sense of the person behind you without looking back. Is it a man or woman, short or tall, smiling or frowning? When waiting for an elevator, ask yourself which door will open first or which floor it will stop at next.

"Always go with your first impression. Don't rationalize. Don't think too much. Just go with your initial gut feeling," Loretta stresses.

Pay attention to your animals and pets, if you have any. Cats and dogs are very sensitive to those who visit us from the other side and to other psychic phenomena. A dog may start barking or move his or her head from side to side as if looking at someone moving or as if hearing sounds you can't hear. Cats may hiss, arch their backs or swat at what appears to be nothing at all. It might be a mouse, a gnat, or a bit of swirling dust.

Then again, it might be something altogether different.

"When you see these signs, engage your own senses and see if you can pick up any images, sensations or emotions. Remember, there are many ways to get information: clairvoyant, clairsentient, claircognizant or clairaudient. There are many tools at your disposal, including Tarot cards, pendulums, dreams, your own imagination and many others. The only way to determine which technique is your best vehicle is to keep practicing to see which one develops into your strongest psychic ability," Loretta says.

You also can get information through different "modalities," such as psychometry. As we've already seen, this is obtaining psychic impressions by holding a piece of jewelry, a photo, a piece of clothing or something that belongs to someone or is associated with the crime at hand. Try this with your friends. Ask them to provide you with an object, then see what information you can pick up. Don't worry about being right or wrong. Developing a psychic gift is like acquiring any other skill. There's a learning curve. The important thing is to keep at it.

"You can build your psychic awareness through a practice called energy reading. You and a friend sit in a chair facing each other, hold hands and see what you can pick up from each other. Your intuitive abilities, and those of your partner, might surprise each of you," Loretta explains.

Here's another exercise.

Flip through the pages of a magazine without looking at the pages, or have someone select a page for you. Make sure that you can't see what's on the page. With your eyes closed, place your hand palm down over the image. See if you can get a "feel" for what that image may be. Just relax. Don't force it, and see what comes through.

Pay attention to what songs pop into your head. Jeanette often gets messages through song. Why is that particular melody or those lyrics flowing through your mind? If The Beatles' *Yellow Submarine* keeps rolling around in your head, perhaps the color yellow is a clue. Perhaps the answer to your problem is submerged in water. Maybe you should go get a sandwich.

Don't laugh. Sometimes your subconscious mind will send you one clue so that you'll stumble across another on the way. Why? Who knows? That's just the way it sometimes works. What could the song's imagery reflect in your current life? How could it apply to the problem, the crime or the missing-person case you're working on? Psychic information is flowing all the time, using all means and methods. Don't cut yourself off from any channel.

There are hundreds of different exercises you can employ on a daily basis. You can even make up your own. The point is to start exercising today and to continue exercising. Be diligent about it. Practice every day and you will be amazed at how quickly and how well your psychic abilities sprout, grow and flower. At some point, you may realize that it's time to start work as a psychic detective.

A warning about Ouija

A lot of people just beginning to develop their psychic abilities gravitate toward the "Ouija board" or even conduct their own séances. It's a natural tendency. Most of us are familiar with at least the concept of the Ouija board from playing with it as children. Some of us as kids even conducted séances for fun.

Psychic detecting is not "fun 'n games." It's serious business, with serious repercussions for those who don't take it seriously. Although a Ouija board or a séance can be a great way to connect with the other side, when you "play," you send an open invitation to all spirits. Although your intentions may be of the highest good and your goal is for only spirits who have love, truth and goodness in their hearts to come through, the person or persons who actually show up may not care about your intentions. As previously noted, those on the other side may have their own agendas and perhaps a very negative agenda.

Some beginners don't seem to care. They want to make contact just for the thrill of it or for the verification. And they don't really care who they contact. That's like jumping into shark-infested waters during a feeding frenzy. It might be exciting, but you probably won't be very happy with the end result.

If you're a beginner, leave these techniques to more experienced practitioners. There are more than enough positive and healthy ways to experience psychic phenomena, test your abilities, and enhance your skills.

Polish your diamond

Loretta compares psychic ability to a diamond. There are four "Cs" to a diamond – cut, clarity, color and carat. Similarly, there are four "Cs" to psychic ability: clairvoyance (seeing), clairaudience (hearing), claircognizance (knowing), and clairsentience (sensing).

Of course, different psychic detectives use different methods to engage those abilities. Some find that images, sounds or sensations just arrive, often unbidden. They might see the flash of an image, perhaps just a flash of color, or just a whiff of a smell or a fleeting sensation. These are those small pieces of the puzzle that can eventually lead to an understanding of the larger picture. Other detectives use a variety of tools, such as Tarot cards, pendulums, dreaming or psychometry.

We'll look at all of these and more in later chapters.

Members of Find Me believe that (1) everyone has some level of psychic ability and (2) that ability can be developed. You are encouraged to start today in developing and enhancing your own God-given psychic abilities.

Commitment, focus, constant practice, and faith in the existence of psychic abilities, in the process or technique the psychic detective chooses to develop, and faith in a higher power are essential. How you see that higher power is your own business. The members of Find Me are psychics, not preachers.

How much should a psychic detective know about a case before he or she begins work? There's no single answer. This is a very individual matter. Some detectives prefer to know little or nothing about the crime, the victim or the missing person.

Jeanette says, "I never read what has been written about the case during the investigation. Otherwise, you'll never know if spirit is giving you the right information or if you're just repeating information you have read."

Others prefer to work with more information, such as birthdays, time of birth, photographs, personal items or items related to the case, and other data. Some create in-depth files. What really matters is what technique works best for the individual investigator. If you need lots of data, that's fine. If you prefer to work "blind," that's just as fine. The best advice is to experiment with both techniques until you know what works best for you.

Trust, but verify

President Ronald Reagan believed in a simple, yet powerful, philosophy when making agreements with other nations – trust, but verify. That's a good rule for developing your psychic abilities. Trust in the fact that the universe is larger, more diverse and more wonderful than we can possibly imagine. Trust that you have the ability to tap into that universe and become a skilled practitioner of psychic art. Trust that you can use those skills and abilities for good. Verify your personal growth by testing yourself, checking your reading and impressions against hard facts, and by referring to your journal.

We all know skeptics who refuse to believe in the incredible wonders that are all around them.

"I'll believe in life after death when Aunt Minnie drops in for a visit."

"I'll believe in clairvoyance when I see a vision showing me the gold in the Lost Dutchman Mine."

"I'll believe in angels when one flutters its wings in my face."

What these disbelievers fail to realize is that we live in a cause-and-effect universe. We have to act to make something happen. We must take a first step if we are to complete a journey. If you've read this far, chances are that you've taken that first step. Be bold. Take heart. Have patience. Always remember, trust your own intuition to create your own pathway of discovery and life fulfillment, and open your mind's eye to a whole new insight on your inner self.

"If I keep a green bough in my heart, the singing bird will come."
-Chinese Proverb

Clairvoyance

with Eileen Nelson

He who knows that power is inborn...and so perceiving throws himself unhesitatingly on his thought, instantly rights himself, stands in the erect position, commands his limbs, works miracles.
~ Ralph Waldo Emerson

Clairvoyance is the ability to see people, objects and events that are not physically present. This psychic vision may appear very real, as if watching something right before your eyes, or it may all take place within the mind's eye. Generally, clairvoyance is what most people think of when they hear the words "psychic ability."

Success: a rosary miracle

A few summers ago, Eileen Nelson received a package in the mail. A friend had sent her a rosary, one ordered from a general-merchandise catalog. Although living in separate states, the friends were very close, having worked together for several years as psychic detectives on unsolved missing-persons and murder cases.

Eileen was stunned at the rosary's beauty. It had clear crystal beads, with the center medal showing a silver carving of St. Bernadette of Lourdes looking up at the Blessed Mother. As Eileen turned it over, she noticed that the plain silver background held water encapsulated at Lourdes, France. She has always appreciated religious articles, and had even had a first-class relic of St. Bernadette given to her by a nun many years earlier. It was an actual tiny piece of the saint's dress, and she had always felt honored to have it.

Eileen placed the rosary in a drawer to keep it safe. Within weeks, her three year-old daughter took it out and broke one of the links. Eileen gently took the rosary and began to sew it back together. Turning over the center piece once again, she now noticed the image of a very holy man's profile, a priest actually, in the holy water/silver background! She was stunned, and wrote her friend about the image.

Eileen began to have religious visions when looking at this image. These visions included the Blessed Mother, the pope, and once even Jesus.

"I thought, 'Either I'm one heck of a psychic, or I'm losing my mind,'" she says. She decided to show the rosary to her friends. Some could see the profile, others had visions, others saw angels and even the Blessed Mother. Some could see nothing at all.

Eileen began to pray the whole rosary faithfully every night, and over time the silver links turned to gold.

"Absolutely fascinating," she says.

About six months later, another package arrived from her friend. She said she had contributed money to a Roman Catholic religious order, the Missionary Oblates of Mary Immaculate and the National Shrine of Our Lady of the Snows in Belleville, Illinois. The package contained a medal of a new saint-to-be, Eugene De Mazenod. The organization was promoting his cause for sainthood. Eileen looked at the medal and almost fainted. The image was the exact profile of the priest's image in the rosary!

Within months, this holy man was canonized and became St. Eugene, patron of the spiritually impoverished. To this day, Eileen has visions in the rosary, and occasionally will show it to someone who hasn't seen it. Often, they have the same reactions.

This is the letter the Missionary Oblates sent when she informed them of this miracle:

Dear Mrs. Nelson,

Thank you for your very interesting letter. I want to thank you also for your support. My Oblate brothers and I are truly grateful for the help you give us. Without the help of persons like you, our ministries would be severely limited.

Also, thank you for taking the time and trouble to write about your experience with your rosary. I would not want you to send it to me to look at for fear it might get lost, and I know that would be very upsetting to you. My limited experience with events such as you described tells me that not everyone is able to see the same things. As you mentioned, some of your friends could see what you saw, and others could not. Perhaps the best way to think of that is as a grace that you received which is a sign that there is a reality beyond what we see with our ordinary vision. That is an essential part of our faith, and if you have had an experience that strengthens your faith, that is a grace. At the same time, it is important that such experiences do not distract us from the primary ways that God is with us, i.e., through the Church and the sacraments.

Thanks again for your letter and your help. Be assured we will continue to keep you and your intentions in our prayers here at the Shrine.

Sincerely in Jesus and Mary,
Fr. William P. Clark, OMI
Director, Missionary Association

A warning – sometimes 'they' don't listen

One of the most famous examples of clairvoyance within the last fifty years was psychic Jeanne Dixon's prophesy that President John F. Kennedy would be assassinated in Dallas, Texas, in November 1963. Dixon, who had a psychic newspaper column for many years and was a well known member of the Washington elite, was already famous by the time she made that fatal prediction.

In fact, she predicted JFK's 1960 presidential victory when the current wisdom and the smart money said his Republican opponent would be the victor.

Three years later, Dixon tried to get a warning to the president (as did many non-psychics), but her efforts, obviously, failed. Her accuracy on this account was amazingly on target. Eileen encountered similar resistance, notably in a case in which she gave clear warning but was ignored by the authorities.

While living in Philadelphia, Eileen got very strong impressions and feelings about the "Mayfair Abductor," the name the media had given a child abductor. The media reported that the abductor was trying to force Catholic school girls into his car. So far, his attempts had been unsuccessful, but concern was rising that he would escalate his efforts into a very dangerous situation. The police were placing undercover officers in the area of Mayfair and Castor Gardens, where Eileen lived at the time.

She called the Philadelphia police. The officer who took her call was delighted to "chat." He listened, then began flirting. Eileen loved the attention, but kept trying to get him to take her seriously. This is a common problem when a concerned psychic detective tries to work with an overly skeptical policeman or investigator. Then she heard another policeman in the background say, "Who the hell are you talking to?" The cop she was speaking with said, "I gotta go," and hung up.

In a week or so, Eileen called the sex crimes unit. A detective came to her house and took her folder of notes and clues. She never heard from him again. After hearing nothing for a few days, Eileen stopped a female officer on the street, figuring that if the men wouldn't listen, maybe a woman would. The officer did, and they met the next day. Eileen was given a sketch of the "person of interest" to study.

They met again at a local pizza shop. A police captain who wanted to see Eileen's evidence turned up as well. Eileen gave them photocopies of what she had originally given the detective from the sex crimes unit. The captain took the material and left.

Eileen had written in those papers that the Mayfair Abductor would have his first successful abduction at the corner of Castor and Magee Avenues. She further predicted that the abduction would be the following Friday morning (providing the precise date) at 7:30. She assumed that the police would station an undercover officer there, as they were doing on some other corners.

Unfortunately, Eileen's clairvoyance was right on target. Even more unfortunately, the authorities didn't listen. That Friday at 7:30 a.m., a Catholic high school girl was abducted at the corner of Castor and Magee Avenues. None of this was picked up by the local media.

To be fair, few policemen, detectives, or search and rescue personnel have studied the world of psychic detecting. Far fewer have had actual experience working with these gifted people. The popular media haven't helped with their inaccurate portrayals over the years, either. Even Jeanne Dixon had her share of strikeouts. For example, she predicted that the United States would have a woman president during the '90s, and that a giant comet would strike the earth during that same period.

These misses bring up an interesting point relating to clairvoyance, and indeed all the tools of the trade used by psychic detectives. Much of the information gathered through psychic work is symbolic. The sights, sounds, smells, tastes and sensations must not only be received and recognized, they must be interpreted. Could it be that the information we receive is accurate, but at times our analysis is flawed? Most psychics will tell you that this is the case. And that's not a cop out. How many ways can one symbol be interpreted or, perhaps, misinterpreted?

For example, suppose you're a psychic detective and your method of research shows you the image of the number four. What does that mean? Could it refer to days, hours, minutes, months or years? Is it an address? An age? Is there a four-leaf clover involved in the case? A regular foursome that plays cards or golf? Could it be an apartment number or the number on a gym locker?

The answer will most likely depend on the detective's personal experience, his or her personal symbols and their individual meanings, and the specific details of the case. You can see how easy it is to receive valid information and still arrive at invalid conclusions. After all, a number of comets *did* come frightfully close to hitting Earth during the '90s. Perhaps Jeanne Dixon was off by a few hundred thousand miles, but considering the size and scope of the universe, that's really not too far off center target, is it?

It's a problem often faced by Eileen, now a member of Find Me and a long time psychic detective.

"The information is not always so 'cut and dry' as picking up a specific name or location. Things will come that don't make sense. At times, I've been hesitant to pass it along because I thought I was wrong, and then it turns out I was right."

This gets back to interpretation and analysis.

It's important that the psychic detective avoid self-editing of the information he or she gets. As psychic detectives, we may be helpful investigators, but we're not an official investigative body. We're not "inside" the investigation, which means we don't get all the inside information the authorities have. Material, data, impressions, visions, sounds or other sensations that seem meaningless to the psychic may be very significant to the authorities. We may indulge in our own interpretations, which may or may not be valid. But we should never indulge in self-censorship. We don't have the inside "scoop," which means we don't have the right to hold back.

The main point for Eileen is to keep on working at the job. When faced with apparently inaccurate readings or an invalid interpretation of the messages received, "the best solution is to just keep on trying," she says.

Often a psychic will receive accurate information right off the bat, and still need to stay on the job. As this book was being written, Eileen was in the middle of just such a case.

Recently, a man named Chris from New York apparently just walked away from his car on a Pennsylvania highway. The keys were still in the ignition when the authorities arrived, but there was no sign of the man. What had happened was a complete mystery. Eileen was contacted by a friend of the family through her website and asked for help.

How this contact came about is an interesting story in itself. Just before getting in touch with Eileen, the woman, Sandy, had hung up a calendar from the Missionary Oblates of Mary Immaculate. A few moments later, she was "surfing the net" looking for help to resolve the case. After looking at a number of sites, she selected Eileen because, when she clicked on the rosary miracle story, she saw the letter about visions Eileen saw in the rosary the Missionary Oblates had sent her. Sandy "just knew" she should make contact based on that coincidence.

Many psychics will tell you that there are no coincidences.

Eileen began working on the case, and soon received information that Chris was alive and not the victim of a murder or serious accident. He had wandered off because he was sick. Sandy wrote back that Chris suffered from schizophrenia. Eileen's husband suffers from the same disorder, and she believes that her familiarity with the illness and her empathy helped her pick up information about the missing man.

A few days later, Eileen received psychic information that Chris had been picked up by a truck driver and that he was still alive. Sandy called right back. Chris's sister had just called. They had just learned about a truck driver who had picked up Chris, given him a ride, and then dropped him off. Unfortunately, Chris had wandered off again.

As of this writing, the family was worried that Chris was out in the elements and suffering from the cold. Eileen believed that he wasn't suffering as much as they thought, and that he soon would be found by the police. This and the previously provided information gave the family considerable comfort in a very trying time.

"This isn't a story about me working a miracle. It's about a real psychic as a real person helping other people in a very real way," says Eileen.

A psychic becomes a psychic detective

"I've always known I was psychic, but reaching out and helping people was something that I just didn't really know how to do," says Eileen.

That's a common obstacle for people with psychic abilities. So how does someone begin a career as a clairvoyant psychic detective? Eileen's advice is basic – just start! How you start depends on your natural abilities, your interests, and the options available in your area.

Eileen found a psychic in her community and started going for visits. Not only did she get valuable readings, she was able to ask questions about the process and see how that process works. Eventually, she felt that reading Tarot cards would be a good place to begin her training.

"I practiced, practiced, practiced until I got really familiar with the cards. I read for family and then friends. After placing an ad in a local paper, I started doing professional readings."

That's how it usually goes. The budding psychic detective conducts research. He or she reads books, visits local psychics who are already "in the business," and then seeks out a niche. That niche may be cards, pendulums, dreaming or any number of valid options. This first major step starts them on an incredible voyage of personal discovery and service to community and humankind.

Eileen is careful to note that a psychic detective can be very successful and still see his or her efforts fail now and again. Exercising psychic ability is more art than science. Information arrives in a variety of ways. As we've said, it's often symbolic and difficult to interpret. Even when the information is valid, our own emotions, belief systems and thought processes can lead to faulty analysis. Add to that the skepticism, and sometimes downright hostility, of the public and many in law enforcement, and you have a recipe for tragedy.

For example, Eileen was working on locating a kidnapper. She predicted the time, date and place of the next kidnapping, which occurred precisely as she saw it. Unfortunately, although the police stationed numerous officers in the general area, none of them was stationed at Eileen's indicated location. She was remarkably successful in getting accurate details of the crime before it happened, but the crime occurred despite her warnings.

The depiction of psychics we see in the movies or on television is frequently overly glamorized. In reality, the experience isn't always a "bed of roses."

For instance, the intense concentration required for her readings caused Eileen to suffer serious headaches. Beyond this, she experienced financial struggles because she did not charge for her readings.

"I figure the Lord pays me, and if adversity comes my way, it's all just part of life, maybe even a test, so to speak." As with many psychics, a certain amount of personal discomfort was a small price to pay for the satisfaction found in helping others.

Networking

When the world famous Chef Emeril wants to really enhance the flavor of one of his recipes, he "kicks it up a notch" by tossing in more spice. That's exactly what Eileen decided to do with her psychic career. She wanted to help more people work through more serious problems, and that led to psychic detecting.

"There is nothing wrong with doing personal readings, but I really wanted to make a difference using my abilities." She "kicked it up a notch."

Like most professionals starting a new career, Eileen began networking. She made contact with a number of psychics, one of whom was also a psychic detective and who asked her to help on a case. As they say at the race track, Eileen was "off and running." The two exchanged clues through the mail, worked on cases, and expanded their network to include other psychics doing the same kind of work.

Finding like-minded individuals, getting to know them, and working with them provides an amazing and essential amount of support.
Psychics are assailed from all corners and are often the butt of cruel jokes and remarks.

Much of this condescension is because of the public's lack of insight and information about the psychic world. Unfortunately, the psychic arena is filled with more than its share of quacks, imposters, phonies, con artists and deluded do-gooders. Legitimate psychics pay a heavy price for the poor judgment and lack of ethical behavior expressed by these individuals. A support group, whether formal or just a few friends, can be of enormous value in enhancing your abilities, expanding your contacts, and in just "being there" when you're hit with the inevitable downside of any endeavor. Besides, you get to meet a lot of great people.

Evolution

Eileen studied, practiced, progressed and eventually decided to become a full-fledged psychic detective, specializing in helping the families of missing, abducted or murdered persons. She did not contact the police authorities in those days, preferring to work directly with suffering families. If they chose to pass along the information to local law-enforcement agencies, that was strictly the families' decision.

"I just jumped in and tried like hell to see if I could come up with anything that would help at all. Just comforting them often was enough to give them renewed hope."

Eileen stays mentally and emotionally alert for clairvoyant messages, which can arrive at any time, any place, and in any state of consciousness. Sometimes names just "pop" into her head. She writes down the information and immediately passes it along to the investigator on the case because time frequently is an important factor.

Self awareness is important because information can come through in so many different ways. Eileen often has visions. They can arrive unbidden or after a session in which she stares at a photograph of the victim, concentrates, and tries to receive a psychic message. These visions are often very vivid and pack an emotionally draining punch.
"But hey, that's part of the territory," she says.

Eileen gets impressions, mental clairaudient messages, and occasionally uses psychometry. As the impressions from psychometry often are rather general, she rarely uses that technique. She advises us to be aware of coincidences in which psychic messages may be hidden. If you hear a name, or a word or see an image again and again in a short period of time, there might be something more to it than coincidence.

For example, if you continually hear a song, over the radio, through a store's music system, on television or in a movie, in an overheard conversation, or even from someone whistling down the street, take a moment to analyze what that song title, lyrics or melody could mean to your investigation. What clue is being handed you? How could it relate to your case? What is the hidden meaning? Is the meaning in the music or the lyrics or both?

How to bungle a case

In the film *Saving Private Ryan*, one of the soldiers in the rescue team is a sniper who uses tracer bullets. Tracers are shells that leave a visible trail when fired so that the shooter can see exactly where his bullets are landing. During a battle scene in which this sniper is picking off enemy soldiers, his buddy shouts, "Remember, tracers go both ways!" He meant that the blazing path of the bullet could just as easily point out the sniper's position to the enemy.

Criminals can be psychic, too – or at least extremely clever. When writing this chapter, Eileen wanted to note some of the dangers overconfident psychic detectives can put themselves in.

One of her earliest cases involved a serial rapist/killer who had left a trail of victims through several states. The killer was a man named Raven (not his real name). She was working with a local sheriff, we'll call him J. Edgar, and two other psychic detectives, Dawn and Raye. They believed that Raven was responsible for killing a number of men and women, but could never find any proof. This was all the more frustrating because Raven lived less than ten miles from Raye's home.

Proximity to the crime and the criminal is no guarantee of successful detecting.

Raye had a clear vision of where to find the body of one of Raven's victims, in the woods near her home. She went to the site and found a fingernail and a pair of pantyhose. Unfortunately neither bit of evidence was able to advance the case. This is another dilemma faced by the psychic detective -- knowing something without being able to prove it.

J. Edgar believed in the psychics, and the team worked well together. They "worked like crazy" to come up with hard evidence, but with no success. Frustration, disappointment and a touch of desperation set in. The psychics on their own decided to "smoke out" Raven and force him into confessing.

Raye knew where Raven lived, and she had an idea about how to "get" him. Her plan was for the psychics to gather as much Roman Catholic literature, such as the pamphlets and flyers handed out by charitable institutions, and flood Raven's home with mail. More than that, they would draw an eye on each envelope as if to say, "We're watching you." The forces of evil were being monitored by the forces of good. Raven would panic, turn himself in, confess, and all would be right with the world.

Eileen prepared her materials and was about to drop them in the mail box when a feeling of fear and dread overcame her. Her instincts virtually shouted that Raven would somehow know where she lived if she mailed that literature. She broke out in a sweat, returned home with her materials and ripped them to shreds. As she finished, a sense of total relief swept over her. It was as if she had "dodged a bullet."

Dawn and Raye didn't hold back. They bombarded Raven's home with the religious literature. Suddenly he knew that "eyes were on him." Naturally, neither psychic used envelopes with return addresses, so that their identities would be protected. They felt safe and secure.

Weeks later, Raye received a package in the mail, a box with no return address. She opened it to find all of the literature she and Dawn had sent out, and a note that read, "I BELIEVE THESE BELONG TO YOU."

That's when Raye and Dawn began sweating bullets. When they told the sheriff what they'd done, he was angry, and understandably so. Raven was a stone-cold killer, and there was no reason to think he'd reformed. J. Edgar pulled all three psychic detectives off the case and insisted that Raye leave town and move far, far away. Fearing for her life, she did so.

The point here is simple. While psychic detecting on one level might be considered "fun 'n games," by some, in the real world we're dealing with real criminals. Some of those criminals are extremely dangerous, amazingly clever, and surprisingly intuitive.

Tracers do indeed go both ways.

Eileen's technique

Pray in. Eileen's religious faith plays a major role in working cases. "The longer I work on missing-person cases, the stronger my faith becomes," says Eileen.

She believes in and practices the power of prayer in her daily life and in her work as a psychic detective. One of her most powerful psychic tools is her rosary. She prays the rosary every night and, when working on cases, often receives messages in the form of visions. She encourages anyone getting into the arena of psychic detecting to embrace and employ the power of prayer.

You'll find this a common thread among most if not all psychic detectives. Even psychics without religious beliefs will take a moment to calm their minds and get in touch with their higher selves, higher consciousness, or their subconscious mind. Whatever your belief system, whatever technique you choose to employ, praying/meditating is an essential first step in the process.

Do a mental review. Eileen runs through any thoughts that have come to her before beginning a case. Frequently, psychics discover that they've been "on the job" before they even know there's a job to be done. Valuable information may have arrived prior to getting, or even knowing, about the case. She invests the time to review information, even so-called wild thoughts, that might now apply to the specific case at hand.

She always makes sure to have pen and paper ready. Information can come at any time and in any place. It pays to be ready to jot down that information. Relying on one's memory is a slippery slope, especially when working multiple cases at the same time. It's better to trust ink and paper, tape recorder or laptop rather than one's memory.

Visualize the client. Eileen carefully evaluates her clients, their mental and emotional state, and their apparent ability to handle the sometimes tragic information she gets.

How should you present information so that it doesn't create false hope? So that it doesn't create a false sense of tragedy? Can this person or family handle straight facts, or must words be couched in softer terms? What will be their response to difficult or even tragic news? Who else is working the case? Are other psychic detectives involved?

Sometimes a victim's family wants the information complete and undiluted, regardless of the content. Other times, they'll "shop psychics" until they find one who will tell them only what they want to hear. Some clients can't handle the truth or the possibility of a sad truth, and fall off the "radar screen" after the first consultation. Eileen believes it's important to know who you're dealing with so you can know how to effectively deal with them.

Engage your skills. Whether seeking a vision, praying her rosary or using psychometry, Eileen consciously engages her skills to begin her research. Even if you are engaged in a relatively passive activity, such as receiving a vision, it's important to be physically, mentally and emotionally prepared. Some psychics call this "setting your intent." Officially beginning and ending a session or series of sessions also helps direct her efforts and keep her focused during the process.

Teamwork. If possible, Eileen likes to work closely with a group of fellow psychic detectives even though different people may come up with entirely different scenarios.

"I feel that all conflicting information should be passed on, since law enforcement may understand things we do not," she says.

Apparent contradictions may not be real contradictions at all to the people who have more information. Additionally, information that makes no sense at present may have important meaning later on as more information becomes available.

For instance, suppose a psychic detective hears the song *Blue Moon* continually playing inside her head, but there's no apparent connection to the case. Later she may discover that a suspect works at the Blue Moon Oyster House, or that an antique blue automobile with baby moon hubcaps was observed near the crime scene, or next month is the annual "blue" moon, or...or...or... All data, whether or not it makes sense at the moment, is significant.

Stay on the job. It's important to keep at the job even when the information is slow in coming or the case appears to be stalled. Eileen tries to make a genuine connection with the individuals and families with whom she works, even when working over great distances through e-mail.

"If they feel comfortable, they'll open up. Cold readings are okay, but it's so much better to have openness between both parties," she says.

Eileen doesn't like to use the telephone for a very practical reason.

"I get headaches when I try to take in everything verbally. When I look at an e-mail, I can take my time without pressure, then get back to that person focused and without painful physical side effects."

She prefers to work slowly, carefully, and precisely, and she strives continually to avoid the psychic version of "pulling the rabbit out of the hat." This isn't magic, she says. It's challenging work. And as with all work, there are good days and bad days, days when you're "hot" and days when your leads turn cold. Consistency and dedication to the task are keys to success.

Provide comfort. Not every psychic detective is mentally or emotionally equipped to provide comfort to a worried or grieving family. As with any group of people, some psychics are outgoing and others are introverted. Eileen has a genuine skill at providing spiritual comfort and guidance. She doesn't hesitate to employ those skills.

"The truth is that many of these cases never get solved, so if I can help a person move on emotionally, I think that's just as valid a contribution as offering clues."

Justified or not, many families in these situations find that law-enforcement officials aren't living up to their expectations. They don't seem as dedicated or concerned as those actors on the television cop shows. That's rarely the actual case, of course, but the police are usually far too busy trying to solve crimes to provide much comfort to the victims or their families. That's just the nature of the situation. Psychic detectives, if they're so inclined, are in a perfect position to fill that gap.

Organize notes. As previously mentioned, Eileen keeps pen and paper handy. More than that, she organizes her notes into files for easy retrieval and reference. She passes along this tip for working with e-mails.

"I always forward the previous e-mail for the sake of efficiency. I can't tell you how many times I had to dig out previous e-mails and review them just to feel I was staying on top of things."

This process may make for lengthy e-mail messages, but it does keep all the information together in chronological order. She also changes the e-mail subject line on each message so that she can quickly and easily tell which message refers to what case. She keeps all her work in an electronic file cabinet on her computer, then backs up those files with hard-copy files, which may also include her notes, newspaper clippings, and other pertinent data.

Avoid jumping to conclusions. The human mind is a wonderful thing. It can find "one and one" and then add them up to achieve two or four or seventeen. When reviewing the facts of a case with the psychic impressions one gets, it's all too easy to create realistic scenarios that may have absolutely no basis in reality. It's also important to avoid the trap of fulfilling a family's unrealistic expectations.

For example, for some reason people would rather hear that their loved one was a murder victim than a suicide. Their pain can be enormous, often overwhelming, and there is a natural desire on the psychic's part to ease that pain. You can do that, she says, and still be an honest and caring psychic investigator.

Eileen uses "kid gloves" when handling cases in which the family is in denial.

"It's important to respond to these heartaches in the most diplomatic way possible. In this business, you have to be a shrink as well as a psychic," she says.

Rule one is to never tell the family or family members outright that you feel their loved one has been murdered or kidnapped or whatever. Eileen makes it a point to state that she can in some cases be wrong or misinterpret the data she receives.

For example, if she picks up that a beautiful young woman is the victim of a serial killer, she just doesn't blurt out that information. She asks the mother what she feels, and if she hears, "I just know my daughter's out there alive, if only we could find her..." Eileen responds truthfully, but in a positive manner.

"You know, I have received information that your daughter might not be alive. But you are her mother, and I always trust a mother's instincts above anyone else's."

This type of response allows the mother (or other family members) the choice of remaining in denial or of moving on and accepting an unpleasant possibility

And who knows, Eileen adds: Mom just might be right.

Be realistic. Sometimes a psychic detective takes a case and starts "hitting on all cylinders" right away. Other cases may be considerably more difficult, and sometimes she might even come up "dry" and can provide no real help at all. Regardless of our skills and abilities, we all have our "off" days. That's just the way life is, and it's no different for psychics.

The key is to remember the good days and all the good we accomplish on those good days. "Keep on keeping on" should be our motto. Even with the off days, you'll accomplish far more in your psychic career by staying on the job than by quitting. You'll find more missing people, solve and prevent more crimes, and help more families by staying on the job than by taking an early retirement.

Fees and rewards

Financial compensation is a very personal matter. Some psychics charge fees for their work. Others accept reward money for a job well done. And still others work *pro bono*, as Find Me does. One way is neither better nor worse than another. It all depends on the individual psychic detective, his or her personal situation, and the case at hand.

Eileen willingly and gladly falls into the *pro bono* category.

"I never charge money on cases because I don't want any feelings of 'this isn't legitimate' to surface. If someone thinks I'm a quack, that's fine. If they think I'm a con artist, that's not fine at all. I find that the Lord pays me somehow, some way for every case I take on. That is enough, so I never worry about the money."

She adds, "Good will win over evil, and I can play one part in accomplishing the good. That's reward enough for me."

Eileen, just like the other members of Find Me, has taken a leaf from Mr. Emerson's book and has unhesitatingly thrown herself on her thought, stood erect, commanded her limbs, and has even worked the occasional miracle.

"It is by logic you prove, but by intuition that you discover."
-Henri Poincare

Clairaudience

with Stephanie Earhart

> *"Every blade of grass has its angel that bends over it and whispers, 'Grow, grow.'"*
> *~ The Talmud*

Clairaudience is psychic hearing. That is, actually hearing words, sounds and messages that are not physically present to the listener. This hearing may arrive in two forms. Sometimes the psychic detective actually hears words, phrases and sentences as if an invisible speaker were present. These messages are hard to miss. It's as if someone standing by your side says, "Look for the missing child at the corner of Lakeshore Drive and Main Street."

At other times, the message comes through in words and phrases, but the message is "heard" within the psychic's mind, something like a random thought. These are more easily missed and can get lost in the clutter of everyday thinking.

In all cases, the psychic detective must remain alert for any information that comes through, regardless of when, where and how. Interpreted properly, these messages are rarely random, and they may contain valid and verifiable information about a crime, or about the fate or location of a missing person.

Music to her ears

Stephanie Earhart practices clairaudience. Some time ago, a woman whose son was missing came to her for help. Stephanie used her abilities, and discovered that the son had passed on. More than that, she established contact with the son, who told her when, where and how he had died. She was able to communicate this information.

In addition, Stephanie provided very personal facts about the young man and his life, information that she could never have discovered on her own, which provided validation for her reading. For example, the son loved to play music. Stephanie could actually hear, in her head, the music he enjoyed.

"When I told the woman he liked to play jazz, she first had to think a moment, and then she responded by saying, 'Oh, my God, he purchased a book of jazz music and had started to play just before his death.'"

'I started out as a child'

A famous routine by comedian Bill Cosby begins with the line "I started out as a child." Of course. We all start out as children! Many psychics begin experiencing their special gifts at a very young age. Frequently they're practicing these abilities before they really understand what's going on. More often than not, a good bit of time passes before they realize that they're the only ones showcasing such talents. Eventually, this can make for awkward moments in school, on the playground or at the dinner table.

"I also read minds and could foretell the future, which scared my classmates half to death," Stephanie recalls.

As with many psychics, Stephanie's abilities emerged early in life.
"I used to scare a lot of my friends by finishing their sentences before they could get the words out of their mouths."

She also could tell what food would be found in another kid's lunch box, what that kid would have waiting for him/her that night at supper, and other facts she couldn't rationally know. If her spirit guides or other spirits happened to be "hanging around," she wouldn't hesitate to speak to them.

Kids being kids, her schoolmates would call her a "witch" or an "alien."

"I soon learned that this wasn't an ability I wanted to show off," she says. Fortunately for Stephanie, Find Me, and the many people she has helped over the years, her psychic skills weren't stifled by peer pressure. She continued to work, study and develop and, as with most children, grow.

In Stephanie's case, she grew into a psychic detective. The information she hears is often very specific, including names, dates and various information.

"When I was young, I spoke to a spirit named Bobby, who taught me how to play stickball, which shocked my teacher and classmates."

Still, growing up was not without encouragement and support.

"I've been lucky. I've had many good teachers who have helped me develop."

Today, Stephanie mixes clairvoyance with clairsentience (psychic feeling), and she sometimes uses Tarot cards.

In her own words, "I am an intuitive psychic and spirit medium as well as an empathy, able to feel and sense what others do. I find it a gift as well as a curse."

She is often aided in her work by spirits who provide information she cannot ascertain on her own. At an early age she recognized an ability to speak with angels, spirits and guides. For example, in her healing work, spirits will speak and provide information on problems or potential problems faced by the person with whom she is working.

"The spirits I contact for others let me feel what these people feel. For example, if a client is having heart problems, I might experience a tightness in my chest and shooting pains down my left arm and leg."

When the student is ready, the teacher arrives

A student can never progress in developing a skill until he or she is ready and willing to commit to that skill. A common thread among budding psychics, among all students really, is that whenever someone is at last ready to transition to a higher level, the right teacher arrives. Help is always on the way. We, as students, just have to make the effort to reach a certain point where our path intersects with that instructor. Psychic ability may be a gift, but serious study and effort is required if we are to fully develop that gift and put it to the highest possible use.

Stephanie began developing her particular skills by using them to help others. She began helping people find missing persons, missing animals and lost objects.

"I love helping others. It gives me a tremendous sense of accomplishment," she says.

Her experiences were a perfect example of on-the-job training. Eventually she reached a level of skill requiring guidance and support for further development. That's when a mentor named Sam arrived.

If you think psychics are mired in a mystical past of dark chambers, cobweb-coated attics, smoky candles, and arcane rituals, think again. Sam arrived through the Internet. Oh, yes, psychics are on more than one information highway.

Sam began sending Stephanie specific challenges and tests online. She'd work on the problem, e-mail the solution and then receive an in-depth critique of her work.

"This was especially helpful because there's a serious difference between getting general advice and in getting specific guidance on a specific problem."

Working on specific challenges is the best way to hone one's skills, she says. You even learn from your mistakes and, over the long haul, you're intuitive abilities are strengthened.

As Stephanie the student progressed (as the child grew), other teachers arrived. She joined a Spiritualist church that encouraged its psychically gifted members to develop their special skills. The church was run by two ordained ministers and a number of internationally known psychics and mediums.

If you begin walking the path of the psychic detective, you will inevitably encounter people with little or no psychic experience who see a conflict between religion and the use of psychic abilities. Most psychics just don't see it that way. In fact, many psychic detectives will be among the most spiritual people you will ever meet. Churches of many faiths, hospitals and hospices, and the general public are beginning to catch on.

Stephanie's church allowed her to develop as a hands-on healer. She even was encouraged to pass along psychic messages she would hear during the services. In addition to providing comfort and support, the church provided an environment in which her psychic abilities could flower. The church also held psychic fairs, and she became an active participant.

"That really started the ball rolling," she says.

Hitting the ball out of the park

"I can tell past, present and possible future events," says Stephanie. "I try to give names, dates and very personal information when I can."

The more specific she can be and the more information not likely to be known by the general public, the more confident in her abilities her clients become.

"One lady I was working with was surprised when I told her about her son who died in a boat accident, and was able to give her on-target information concerning her son. Many accurate messages came through," she says.

Stephanie can often describe people her clients know or whom they will meet shortly. To do so isn't just performing a parlor trick. Rather, providing such accurate and detailed information helps the client realize that he or she is truly working with a legitimate psychic who has his or her best interests at heart. Confidence allows them to be not only more comfortable with Stephanie and the psychic process, but it also puts them at ease so they can participate more fully in that process.

When asked to predict the outcome of a situation, she can do so, but with a careful admonition. The information she gets about a possible future is never set in stone.

"We have free will, and every choice we make changes the future," she says.

Finding lost children has always been a focus of Stephanie's work, and finding Find Me has helped her gain even more focus.

"This group has given me the opportunity to stretch myself," she says.

Sometimes the people Stephanie finds are beyond help from the physical world, yet her work allows her to assist the family and friends of the missing and deceased deal with the loss. For example, she was asked to help locate a missing young woman. Stephanie made contact, listened to her voices, and shared the fact that the girl had passed on. More than that, she was able to provide the location where the body could be found. Although this was a tremendous shock to the family, just knowing the truth and finding the deceased's body provided important closure to a sad incident.

Stephanie's technique

How does someone become a clairaudient or, for that matter, how does someone acquire psychic ability?

Stephanie answers with another question. "How do some people acquire their tremendous musical abilities? It's a gift from God." She goes on to note that it is the individual's responsibility to develop that ability and put it to the best possible use.

Spirit voices play a major role in Stephanie's work, but that arena has its own challenges.

"You just can't dial up 1-800-SPIRIT and expect an answer over your psychic telephone."

Stephanie engages in a true partnership to get spirit messages. Everything in the universe vibrates. Rocks, plants, animals, humans and spirits all vibrate, but at different frequencies, she says. The more advanced, if that's the proper word, the higher vibration. For example, a human vibrates at a faster rate than a rock. A spirit vibrates faster than a human, and so on. The spirits lower their level of vibration while she raises her level so that "we meet in the middle." This middle ground is where the communication occurs. That's where she hears her messages.

She also helps people contact their personal guides and angels, and gives their names and information. Names? That's right. Stephanie says, "Angels don't often have names. They show me the number that's around a person and appear to me using colors. Sharing these gifts gives me a sense of genuine satisfaction."

There is a price tag.

"This takes a lot of energy on both our parts, and can be physically draining."

It's a price she's more than willing to pay, however. The rewards far outweigh the cost of admission.

Stephanie has the ability to telepathically communicate with animals, much like the famous Dr. Doolittle in the movies. Once, she encountered a dog that wasn't eating his food. Its owner was terribly worried that the poor animal had contracted some disease. When Stephanie communicated with the animal, she got a not-too-surprising answer. He didn't like the way it tasted. She told the owner, who immediately changed the diet, and the dog began eating again.

This ability makes more sense than the average skeptic might believe. After all, animals have brains, and animals can clearly understand and respond to human speech. "Fetch!" "Come here, girl." "Good, dog." It's just as clear that the communication is a two-way street. Ask pet owners if their animals can communicate wants and desires – especially around meal time. Why shouldn't animals be able to communicate telepathically with someone open to receiving the messages?

An encouraging word

Stephanie believes that psychic ability is a God-given talent and that, to some degree, God gives us all a psychic talent. She states that we share a responsibility to develop and enhance that ability, to use it for our own personal advancement and for the greater good of humankind. She advises continual study and practice. She encourages people developing their skills to seek out, learn from and be inspired by talented psychics who are already practicing their skills. Their friendship will be more than a stepping stone to greater awareness; it will be a true blessing. We've all had our moments in which intuition has proven correct.

"All psychic ability is one step above intuitive abilities, and we can all develop these abilities if we want to. As a teacher, I love to learn new things. Life without growth is stagnant.

"What lies behind us and what lies before us are tiny matters compared to what lies within us."
-Ralph Waldo Emerson

Clairsentience & Psychometry

with Joanne Miller

"The work of an unknown good man has done is like a vein of water flowing hidden underground, secretly making the ground green."
~ Thomas Carlyle

Physical objects often retain information about the people, places and events associated with that object. "Reading" that information by holding an item and sensing those impressions is called psychometry. It's a form of clairsentience, the ability to sense what's not detected by the five senses.

A good analogy would be the ability of a trained bloodhound to track down a criminal or missing person. The dog is shown an item known to be handled exclusively by the person being sought. The bloodhound's olfactory abilities allow it to differentiate this individual to the exclusion of others The animal's sense of smell is so acute that it can track that scent over great distances, even over water. There's nothing really mystical about it: The animal has been trained to use this unique ability.

A psychometrist does the same thing, only he or she employs psychic abilities instead of an olfactory sense to transfer information. The psychic detective holds an object and senses information associated with that object. Often, he or she doesn't have to know what it is or even have to look at it. Sometimes the information coming through is rather general or symbolic. At other times the information can be quite detailed and specific.

Again, it's not really mystical. The detective just happens to have developed a particular skill above and beyond normal human experience. Most psychics believe we all have such talents. It's just that some of us are unaware of them or are unwilling to develop them.

Joanne Miller is a member of Find Me who practices psychometry. Like the other members, she seeks neither fame nor fortune for her work. And, like the unknown good man quoted above, she and the other members use their skills and abilities quietly and with dedication to "make the ground green" and help improve the lives of their fellow humans.

Validation sought, validation found

Joanne was living in Oklahoma when she heard about Ruth Davis, who conducted past life regressions. Fortunately, Joanne knew someone who knew Ruth and was able to arrange a meeting. Joanne discovered that Ruth was conducting evening classes in psychometry. Not even certain of what the word meant, Joanne signed up, and she soon found herself swapping rings, keys, watches and other personal items with members of the class.

Most people in the class were just average folks, normal people with an interest in psychic phenomena. Apparently, none of them really expected to achieve much with psychometry. Joanne notes that they were all in for a surprise. Ruth gave each class member pen and paper and told them to write down any impressions they received about the object they were to read. She also suggested that they hold the object close to their hearts or their "third eye." The third eye is located in the center of the brain, and it acts as an access point for sending and receiving psychic information. Touching an object to the center of your forehead will enhance the ability of your third eye to pick up those impressions.

Joanne was working with Ruth's ring and, when it was her turn to speak, she shared the message she had received.

"I got 'illness' and 'leg,'" she said. Ruth, whom Joanne had met for the first time that evening, said that she did have a leg problem. Many years earlier, she had been in an automobile accident that resulted in one of her legs becoming shorter than the other. That was enough validation for Joanne. She was off on a lifetime of psychic adventures.

Paranormal is normal

Joanne says, "A psychic is a normal person with extraordinary gifts." Unlike many psychic detectives, Joanne didn't discover her innate ability until she was an adult. Spared the trauma of being a child psychic, she grew up to become a wife, mother and grandmother. She says that nothing in her appearance would indicate anything other than a normal person, but nothing could be further from the truth.

"If I'm to be considered normal, then you have to consider the fact that I talk to the dead, see visions of things to come, converse with aliens, diagnose illnesses without any medical training, and receive information about people simply by holding something they've touched."

Adult education

Joanne was leading a very ordinary adult life – normal – when the first inkling that she possessed extraordinary gifts arrived. She had worked as a nanny, a veterinary receptionist, and as a housekeep "ER," and her life revolved around her family. Joanne had never even considered the possibility that she might someday become a psychic, much less a psychic sleuth. Things changed when she saw a television program featuring Ruth Montgomery speaking about automatic writing and past life regressions. Intrigued, Joanne decided to give automatic writing a whirl.

She put pen to paper and waited. And then she waited some more. Just before she was about to chuck the paper into the nearest trash can, her pen began to move. After a few nonsense scribbles, the word "Louise" formed. She asked Louise to say something about herself.

Louise started communicating, saying that she had lived in Charleston, Virginia (now West Virginia), and that she and her children had been killed by Indians in 1608. Joanne was surprised at how quickly and easily the information flowed. Later, she tried to interest her husband in the event, but he proved to be somewhat less communicative than Louise. When she confided in her brother, who was very religious, he cautioned her in no uncertain terms against continuing her paranormal pursuits. She complied, but as a fisherman might say, "The hook was set."

A police call

Joanne continued with her studies of psychic phenomena, especially psychometry. She practiced regularly and began to give readings to individuals and families. As her skills improved, she realized that she had much to offer a larger community. She decided to become a psychic detective.

How does one become a psychic detective? Joanne went straight to the source by calling her local police department.

"Luckily, the officer I spoke with gave me a chance to prove myself by making an appointment for me to meet one of the detectives on the force," she says. "I felt that if I could meet with them and if they were encouraged by what I could show them psychically, they just might let me work on some of their cases."

To some, that might sound like a long shot, but it was a shot that hit the target. She met with detectives, explained her gifts and what she could offer, and they came up with a method to see if they could work together on a long-term basis.

"Once I was accepted as a person who would be reliable and responsible, I found I could give information that indeed helped in solving crimes."

This is an important point that shouldn't be overlooked. Investigative personnel are generally skeptical about psychic detecting, and even those who accept the concept must walk on eggshells when working cases that way. Psychic information isn't admissible in court. Psychics are often viewed as frauds, con artists or deluded do-gooders. Even the most sincere psychic will face skepticism and sometimes outright hostility. The more normal the psychic appears and acts, the better his or her chances of establishing, building, and maintaining a sound relationship with the authorities.

A psychic detective wearing a suit and tie will find a more open reception than a psychic wearing a cloak and a turban. Like it or not, that's just the way things are. Most psychics look pretty much like everybody else anyway. You couldn't pick one out of a group of people just by looking at the way he or she dresses and acts.

Some, however, like to dress up. Perhaps wearing more exotic clothing or jewelry is "part of the act," a marketing tool, or maybe he or she just likes the exotic look. That's all well and good, but if you want to become a credible psychic detective, you must ask yourself which is more important – an exotic image or enhanced opportunities to help your fellow humans?

A wakeup call

Joanne encourages interested psychics to explore the possibility of putting those talents to work in psychic detecting. The rewards are enormous. She also notes that the role of the psychic detective is not without its hassles, frustrations and even dangers. Again, the world is full of skeptics, especially in law enforcement, and you really can't blame them for that skepticism. Although we all have some psychic ability, few of us recognize it, and fewer still develop and use it. Suddenly someone comes along and says that she can help solve the crime just by handling the missing man's watch.

"Oh, really!"

The psychic has to develop a thick skin. More importantly, she has to develop a willingness and a desire to help others, regardless of the hurdles some people in the community set up. The greater good is always the greater goal.

Physical, mental and emotional danger frequently come with the package. Even the best psychic can never be absolutely certain from whom or from where unexpected dangers will arrive. For example, Joanne was working on a murder case when she accidentally encountered the man who had murdered his wife. She had volunteered to help out on a case in which a woman left home, but never arrived at her destination. Joanne met with the woman's daughter in the missing woman's home. She held a number of objects and began to get impressions. She received a clear picture of the killer, whom she immediately described.

"You just described my step-dad!" said the daughter. She added, "And he's outside mowing the lawn right now!"

Fortunately, the stepfather didn't believe in psychics, and a precarious situation was avoided.

"After that, I decided to be more careful about what role I played in these investigations. I started paying attention to how I could keep myself out of danger," Joanne says. She finds that working online with individuals and groups, such as Find Me, is the ideal means for psychic detecting.

"It's the perfect scenario, and it proves that psychics and law enforcement can work side by side."

Joanne's technique

"Once I started doing psychometry, other areas opened up to me," says Joanne. These areas include receiving glimpses of future happenings, medical intuitive abilities, and speaking with spirits and spirit guides. Her process is basic, but effective.

Find a quiet space. Joanne's favorite quiet space is anywhere she can be isolated from disturbing sounds. Even the bathroom will do. It's important to have a place in which there are as few disturbances and distractions as possible. Any interruption in your environment will probably disrupt the flow of information or at least make the process more challenging, she says.

Each psychic detective must find his or her own special quiet place. It can be a special room set aside for just that purpose, or any room in the house that can be secured for a time to do this type of work. A den, bedroom, workroom, or even the kitchen table (after everyone has left the house) will work fine. Some psychics find their quiet places outdoors in the forests or nearby parks, lakes or recreational areas.

Whatever works for you is what is best for you – and the missing people and victims of crime. Even when you're on the road on vacation or on a business trip, a little looking around will produce a quiet area in which you can work. Find it and put it to good use is Joanne's advice.

Prepare for the session. In addition to providing a quiet place to work, Joanne prepares that place for work. The cell phone is turned off and, as far as possible, all distractions are circumvented. She makes sure to have plenty of writing paper and functioning pens handy. Other psychic detectives may prefer to use their laptop computers, a typewriter or personal tape recorder. Experiment to find the best, most accurate and most efficient tools and methods for your skills, then employ them for the highest possible good.

Practice. Although she is an experienced practitioner of psychometry, Joanne continues to hone her skills, improve her technique and seek out new and betters ways to help other people through her talents. You'll find this trait among the best in all professions. The better they are, the better they want to become, and the more they're willing to work at it.

Practice is a regular part of Joanne's routine.

Engage. She begins her sessions by holding the provided object or objects. She holds them comfortably, moving them around gently so that she gets a good feel for the entire object. This movement is important because different impressions can be picked up from different areas or parts of the object.

"I've discovered, for instance, that holding eyeglasses one way gives me a view of the person wearing them. Holding them the opposite way provides information on this person's surroundings."

Any object that the missing person, victim or even the perpetrator has touched can be used for psychometry: a toothbrush, a pen, a set of keys, sunglasses, virtually anything a person has handled regularly will do. "Watches and jewelry work very well for me," she says.

When the session begins, Joanne relaxes and allows the images and impressions to come in. She records them immediately so they won't be lost or become confused through memory loss over time. This is extremely important. Many psychics who provide valid information while "in the flow" often can't remember that information, or they remember it imperfectly shortly after their sessions. Data gathering is important. It's just as important to retain that data so it can be put to use. Don't pre-judge the validity of any information you receive. Even if it makes absolutely no sense to you, it might be very important to the person you're reading for.

A final thought

While wrapping up her comments on this chapter, Joanne was reminded of a poem she had written in 1985, a verse that perfectly describes what compelled her to help find missing persons and help the victims of crime.

Words that would if come to me, settle gently on my page,

as if by magic in my head.

Find Me

Dancing ever in my mind, whirling thoughts arrive on time.

Whose creation are they though? By chance they're yours?

You never know.

Pending, waiting, subtly, creeping forward until they're spawned.

*Hatching, popping, onward, outward, come the message fully
formed.*

Eloquently, lavishly, appointed as they be, expressed with deep affection,

Roared with welled emotion. Come these chosen words to you, to do,

The very thing we spew.

The object you say, to give us life among the living
.
To cut us free into your world. Our hand you see stretched out to thee.

To grasp, to tell, but never quell.

*Disguised, enwrapped, unheeded though they be, at times it almost flows
out endlessly.*

We make the mold, we give it life. We give it sound, our voice abounds.

Though countless times, the words fall unheard, unsung, a labor lost.

*These words that would have bridged the gap, are once again held under
wrap.*

Tap the source, give it full flight, prepare to wander where we lead.

Use our thoughts we enter in, these seedlings that we sow, begin.

*Truth will ultimately prevail where there are plans taken to bring it to
light.*

~ George Washington

Claircognizance

With Nancy Marlowe

"The real magic lies not in seeing new landscapes, but in having new eyes."

Dear Kelly,

Thank you again for all of your group effort in locating my brother. I wish I had had the foresight to contact you earlier in the week....

This letter continues to describe how Find Me helped locate a missing motorcyclist in South Carolina. Nancy Marlowe was particularly helpful in that search. Her clues, and those from other members, pinpointed the spot were the body of the missing man was found.

Among the "hits" Nancy had were: He was deceased. He was the victim of an accident and not foul play. His body would be found near a specific highway on the way to a specific town. He had suffered head trauma. His body would be found in a wooded area with a lot of leaves, and near a pond. He was cold at the time of the accident (the weather that day was in the 50s).

All these clues were provided in writing to Find Me's Kelly Snyder, who forwarded them to the family and the proper authorities. All panned out when the man's body was eventually found.

In many cases, Find Me is called in after the fact, often well after the fact, and the group has participated in a number of "cold cases." While the desired conclusion, finding someone alive and well, is sometimes impossible, Find Me is able to help bring closure to grieving families. The "thank you" letters, calls and e-mails from grateful families and friends are all the compensation that members of Find Me could ever want.

Communication is a two-way street

Psychics often hear the question, "How do you know what you know?" The answers are as varied as the people who answer the question. Some see people, places and events. Others hear them, feel them, or in some way get impressions and information through paranormal channels. People blessed with this ability just know things. Universal Intelligence communicates powerfully 24/7, but we have to be willing to listen if we want to get the message.

Communication is a two-way street. There must be a receiver as well as a sender. Key to developing psychic ability and to using it effectively is to be a willing receiver, realizing that information is coming in all the time, and in very many and sometimes unexpected ways. It's important to, as much as possible, be an open channel to the information that will inevitably come your way.

The claircognizant 'toolbox'

Claircognizance is the ability to just "know" something about some person, place or thing without making an effort. In a very real sense, the only "tools" you need are an open mind and a willingness to participate in the process. This information can be accurate even if the psychic hasn't studied, read about, been to, or met the subject of the case at hand. For example, Nancy describes having, from childhood, a "protective radar" that can pick up honesty, dishonesty, ill will and so on in other people. Without thinking, she just "knew" whom she could and couldn't trust.

The messages may arrive without effort, but that doesn't mean the process is easy. Because this "knowing" arrives in the same manner as a normal thought, it's often hard to distinguish between the two. A psychic message may "sound" just like the normal "chatter" that clutters most of our minds. If a psychic is to use claircognitive abilities, it's essential to learn to distinguish one from the other. One must learn to experience and trust the information that comes in. Achieving that awareness takes patience and practice

The process

The process varies from person to person, but it's fair to say that there is little if any process involved. Some psychics are just aware of information without effort. The messages just arrive. Some receive messages all the time, even while performing everyday tasks such as driving to the store, cleaning a room or taking a shower.

All one really needs is to open up to receiving psychic information. The information is there all the time. If this is your skill, all you need is the willingness to accept the gifts the Universe sends. In the case of psychic detecting, those gifts may be the life of a child or at least closure for a grieving family.

Never observe, judge, dwell or doubt

As Nancy says, "I 'just know' about things I have never studied or even heard about. For example, upon meeting someone, I 'just know' whether or not that person has cancer."

Jacquelyn and Nancy advise people trying to develop this skill to "just do it" and to avoid thinking too much about the subject or the process. In claircognizant "knowing," the more you involve your thoughts, emotions, judgments and observations, the less you will come to know. Not only will you be filtering the information, you will be altering it. It's important to just allow yourself to acquire information that's as unfiltered as possible, then file it with the appropriate person or organization.

Don't push the river

When you try your hand at psychic detecting, remember the last words in that last paragraph. Sometimes, very clear and important information may not make any sense at the time it arrives. It's important to record and pass along all the information, regardless of how you feel about that information at the moment. Psychics rarely get the full picture and are often kept "out of the loop" by professional investigators. Even if the information makes absolutely no sense to you, it may connect some important "dots" for the investigators. When you hold back, you might hold up the investigation.

Every new psychic investigation provides you with a learning opportunity and an opportunity to practice and enhance your abilities. Like playing a musical instrument or any creative endeavor, practice perfects performance. Patience is a key asset as cases tend to be resolved when the time is right. Many people don't believe we are human beings with immortal souls. Rather, we are immortal souls who are having a temporary human experience. Immortal souls obviously have a different take on time than we "mere mortals."

Many psychic detectives will tell you that even the vilest crime can serve a higher goal. How can rape, murder and horrible incidents possibly serve a higher purpose?

Understanding. Resolution will follow when the participants come to a new understanding of themselves and their very important place in the universe. That's a very difficult concept for many people to accept, yet it's one many psychic detectives have come to embrace.

How does a psychic detective convey this type of information? The consensus seems to be that the psychic has to take each situation on its own merit. Some people are stronger than other people. Some can handle difficult concepts, and some just aren't willing to "go there." The goal of the psychic detective is to seek the most positive outcome possible.

Again, you never know how important information may show up. As a psychic detective, you may know something that's extremely important. Yet, logically, at that moment it makes no sense at all. Knowing can be experienced as a realization, as a feeling, as a thought, a sound, a taste, and even a smell. It's essential that the detective keep an open mind. He or she should always consider the possibility that an event, thought or feeling may have far more significance than it may appear to at the moment.

It is very beautiful here, if one only has an open and simple eye without any beams in it. But, if one has that it is beautiful everywhere.

-Vincent Van Gogh

Meditation

with Amanda Schell

> *We are members of a vast cosmic orchestra in which each living instrument is essential to the complementary and harmonious playing of the whole.*
> *~ J. Allen Boone*

Some of the "music" from that cosmic orchestra plays out in the form of information about crimes, criminals and missing people. If you're interested in investigating such cases, it's important that you listen to that famous "still, small voice," the one inside your head that feeds you unexpected, but important, information.

One of the best ways to hear, interpret and use those noises is to go inside your head through meditation, a technique successfully practiced by the authors of this chapter. Amanda Schell has called the experience an "extraordinary journey into spiritual awakening."

Meditate on this

Meditation is an ancient technique used for relaxation and rejuvenation, spiritual awareness, revelation and, by some people, for psychic detecting. How far back into human history the practice goes is unknown, but it's likely that our remote ancestors, their Neanderthal cousins, and other long-gone members of the human family tree were doing a lot more than roasting marshmallows when they stared into the evening fire.

Your local library and favorite bookstore will certainly have a number of good books on the subject, and there's probably someone in your community teaching one of the techniques.

Different types of meditation are available for different uses and effects.

In one, the practitioner seeks to eliminate all thoughts and emotions, stilling the mind as much as possible to achieve total peace. Another version seeks to connect with God, the Goddess, the Universe, the Great Mystery, or whatever fits his or her belief system. Still another form concentrates on a person, place or thing to gain insight and information about the fate of that person, place or thing. You will read about, and should experiment with, two proven and effective meditative processes in this chapter. But first, let's get a little background on our psychic detectives.

Amanda's story

"I have always felt a strong spiritual connection, a connection that has always been independent of any particular religion or philosophy," says Amanda.

She was an adopted child, a fact she didn't learn until reaching age 33. Raised by Jewish parents in a loving household, she was encouraged to be creative, athletic and independent.

Amanda didn't undergo the stressful childhood experiences many psychics encounter because her abilities surfaced only after sustaining a serious neck injury at the age of 32. Radical surgery was called for, including the removal of two cervical discs, a bone graft, and a spinal fusion held together by screws and a titanium plate. Unfortunately, the surgery failed, and she spiraled into intense, chronic pain and hopeless despair. Fortunately, her traumatic experiences led to great spiritual advancement, the ability to help others in crisis, and serious work as a psychic detective.

Before that work began, Amanda hit bottom. Spiritual, yet not religious, she knelt and prayed for wellness and relief with "the most soulful of prayers."

Things began to happen – fast.

"I found myself completely bathed in an incomprehensible light of love and energy of divine origin. My prayer was answered with a full-blown illumination experience, from which I emerged with great joy, fulfillment and a sense of the unlimited nature of the human spirit."

Amanda felt optimism well beyond anything she had experienced as a child or youth. Better than that, she learned that she could recreate her enlightenment experience every day.

The pain from her injury and her surgery remains, "yet the love and illumination from these experiences sustain me with a persistent joy, an awakened consciousness, and heightened psychic sensitivities."

It seems that the universe is not a zero-sum plane of existence. Loss is balanced by gain. Anguish and pain can lead to spiritual and personal enlightenment. Of course, one must be willing to look beyond the agony to find the ecstasy.

Amanda's technique

Again, there are many meditation techniques available and, if you desire to become a psychic detective, you should experiment to determine which form best suits your personality, lifestyle, environment and purposes. In fact, Amanda uses a variety of techniques. That being said, a good place to begin your experiments is with Amanda's basic process, which combines dream-meditation with traditional meditation techniques.

The dream team

When receiving an assignment from Find Me, Amanda begins to facilitate her meditations by making preparations the prior evening. She takes pen and paper and writes down a number of questions relating to the case. She then asks her guides for help and for specific information. Having set her intention, she can then clear her mind, go to sleep, and let the process (and the guides) begin.

"Upon waking, I review my dreams and look for messages that are in any way consistent with my questions." She uses the same note pad to write down any specific information, impressions or images recalled from the previous night's dreams. She then gets up, splashes a little water on her face, opens the curtains to fill her room with sunlight, and then returns to the notepad. Most of her dream information is random and not very case-specific. Still, it can be very valuable. Everything is recorded.

Silencing the 'chatterbox'

The process continues. Amanda writes down more questions relating to the case and then starts meditating. Splashing water on her face and opening up the room helps her enter a meditative state without returning to a dream state. Again, she uses a variety of techniques borrowed from books and tapes.

"But I always begin by trying to eliminate any kind of left-brain rational chatter to ensure that the information I receive is coming to me and not from me."

Left-brain chatter is a problem for many psychics, and truly, anyone trying to concentrate. Amanda has solved the problem by putting her left brain into a mental lock box.

"As I begin meditation, I do some deep breathing. Then, by visualizing the left side of my brain, I visually dissect it, and gently slide it into a holding container. Then, I put three locks on it."

It's just a mental exercise, but an effective means of separating the left brain from the process. If you're squeamish about dissecting your own brain, visualize locking it in a closet, another room, a wall safe or a toy box where it will be safe and secure until you need it again. The process may sound silly to some, but you'd be unwise to ignore the power of imagination in helping you enter a meditative or psychic state.

After mentally locking away her logical mind, Amanda thinks "stop talk now…enter spirit."

She finds that the chatter is instantly eliminated, and she can enter her deep, spiritual state.

"Any questions that need to be asked to gather more information on a case while I am in this deep meditative state, are asked by my true higher self," she says. She believes that the process has no place for rational thinking or questions since the information received is, at times, seemingly irrational and non-logical.

"If the left side of my brain were actively involved, a natural tendency would be to eliminate and edit the irrational and seemingly non-logical information gathered, resulting in a loss of potentially valuable information. I have learned to document everything and edit nothing! This is really the only way to be true to this process and honor the accurate information that spirit so graciously delivered to me."

Clearing

At this point, Amanda is immersed in spiritual essence and can begin the next step. She progressively opens and clears her "chakras" by visualizing the colors associated with each. Chakras are specific sites within the human body through which energy flows. They have been used since ancient times in Chinese and Indian medicine. There are seven key charkas, each one associated with a specific color:

• Crown chakra (divine crystalline white light lined with vivid violet) located at the top of the head

• Sixth chakra (indigo) on the forehead above the bridge of the nose

• Throat chakra (blue) at the throat

• Heart chakra (emerald green) in the chest area between the breasts

• Third chakra (bright yellow) in the area of the navel

• Sexual chakra (orange) roughly halfway between the navel and the genitals

• Base chakra (red) on the perineum between the anus and genitals.

Chakras are far too complex a subject to take on here, but there are numerous books, tapes, CDs, Internet sites and other forms of information readily available if you'd like to study the subject.

"I recommend going to your favorite book store and letting the book, tape or CD pick you! Your intuition is the best tool in discovering techniques that will be most effective for you," says Amanda.

One of her regular meditations is called "The Mystic Marriage," in which she opens and stimulates her "third eye." She begins by visualizing her third eye, first on the surface of her forehead.

"Then I see this center opening deep into the center of my brain where the pineal gland is located."

This gland is known as a vestigial sensory organ which many believe is the source of the third eye. She visualizes this center as a perfect circle, like a medium pea shape. She then "sees" her third eye moving in a 360-degree rotation, up, down, front, behind and side to side. Amanda believes this is the real center of her strong clairvoyant sense. After warming up with a few more rotations, she focuses her third eye on looking straight up to the spirit world, staring directly until she sees and connects with what she calls the "Universal Eye."

When this direct connection is achieved, she can begin to elevate spiritual energy, synchronizing her rate of vibration until it's in harmony with the spirit world. Some spiritualists refer to this as "the quickening."

Take off

The power of imagination plays a major role in the work of many psychic detectives. Medical science is learning what psychics, hypnotists, healers, and shamans have known for generations. One of the greatest forces on planet Earth is the power of a focused human mind.

In the next to last step of her process, Amanda knows she's on the brink of the spirit world. She's nearing her destination and, hopefully, some answers on the case.

"I visualize a sort of hand-held lever, something like the stick an aircraft pilot uses to control the motion of an airplane. I hold onto this handle and push it upward until a monitor above me reads 'ON.'"

Mentally, emotionally and spiritually she has reached take off.

Landing

"The last step before becoming fully immersed in spirit occurs when I visualize a sliding trap door," Amanda says. "When I gently slide it to the left, I open this awesome divine portal which fills me with bright, bright crystal heavenly light."

She has "landed" in the spirit world.

She begins work by connecting with her spirit guides. Sometimes she meets victims involved in her cases who have passed on. She does not verbally repeat the questions she has previously written down.

"I open the question as if opening a door through which I can receive the information I'm seeking."

The information comes in different forms, sometimes in random bits and pieces, and sometimes it unfolds as if she's watching a movie or television show. In the latter case, "I can begin to ask even more specific questions during the 'film.'"

For example, during one meditation, she clearly saw a north-south highway running parallel to the Atlantic Ocean. She saw that and nothing more. But with that information, she was able to ask her guides for more specific details, such as the number of that highway, during the next meditation.

The meditative state can allow this information to come forward in any number of ways.

"When I'm in deep meditation, I can see an event (clairvoyant), I can hear names and voices (clairaudient), and I can sometimes feel the sensations felt by the victim or lost individual (clairsentience)."

Experience has shown that Amanda is primarily clairvoyant, with secondary clairaudient and clairsentience sensations.

Giving thanks

Amanda always offers deep thanks and sincere gratitude to the spirit realm before returning to the physical world. Then she can complete her meditation and end the session.

"I close the sliding trap door and then gently pull back the control lever until my monitor reads 'STAND BY.' I then begin to return to the physical world through an energy spiral."

She begins with the color white and descends through all the colors of the chakras until she feels her mind has fully returned to her body. She then frees her left brain from its temporary lockbox.

Again, these visualizations are key to the success of the techniques used by many psychic detectives. There's nothing magical about imagination. We all have imagination. Psychics (and others) just harness that power and put it to good work. Find out what mental images work best for you, then employ them in your psychic work.

Amanda finishes the process by taking three deep breaths of "divine white light" in through her nose and out through her mouth. She begins to become aware of physical sensations, wiggles her fingers and toes, and she stretches her whole body.

"I open my eyes, read a daily affirmation, followed by a prayer of gratitude for the information I've been provided."

She immediately gets back to pen and paper to jot down everything she's experienced through her spiritual senses. If any visuals have been particularly strong, she'll sketch them out before turning in her report to Find Me.

Amanda encourages anyone practicing meditation to, well, practice meditation.

"The more times I practice my meditations, the better I become at refining my questions and receiving answers that are accurate and useful."

That last comment is particularly important. As much as psychic detectives enjoy, become immersed, or are spiritually and emotionally affected by their experiences, the good ones realize there are very practical goals involved in this paranormal work. – finding missing people and solving crimes.

Still, the experiences and rewards one encounters with and in the spirit realm can be awesome.

"Every time I experience my deep meditation, I feel that I am 'coming home,' the home I came from and the sweet home I will return to one day. Nothing can complete me more than the deep, deep love and divine gratitude and appreciation for all that I have been blessed with. It includes the desire to fulfill my highest and greatest purpose here in the physical world and to truly open my heart to care and share, to live and give with love," she says.

"When all is said and done, all we really have of any grand importance is love. All my meditative activity is guided by these intentions, and the realization that the bonds of love are unbreakable and truly invincible. I prefer not to refer to the psychic casework as work. Rather, I perceive it as service, a great service I am providing by using this God-given ability to make a universal difference. My energies and efforts in this service are always rooted in my deep desire to be of help to those in need. I'm motivated to assist in any way possible to right a wrong. I'm deeply driven to contribute to making our world a kinder and safer place for all living creatures."

Developing your meditation skills

Anyone can meditate, and more people than you might think practice this skill. The private "coffee breaks" or "naps" or "quiet moment" taken by businesspeople, by government and organization leaders, are actually brief moments of meditation. People with stressful occupations have learned the value of meditation in reducing stress, restoring balance, and promoting a more physically, mentally, emotionally, and certainly spiritually balanced life. The technique also can be used to find missing people. Here are a few suggestions if you would like to begin meditation.

First, you can find any number of books, CDs, tapes and DVDs at your library or favorite bookstore. Make the investment and start practicing the various techniques until you find one that works best for you. CDs and audio tapes are recommended to beginners by some Find Me practitioners. The listener, even a beginner, can be easily guided on an incredible and incredibly peaceful and insightful experience. Meditation teaches you to quiet your mind and listen to the feelings and thoughts that are messages from the paranormal.

Again, it's important to journal your experience, so always have pen and paper nearby. Like dreams, these insights can be fleeting experiences, regardless of their importance.

Meditation is so simple, yet so effective, that it's an excellent place for a novice to begin experiencing his or her psychic gifts. Once you enter the paranormal world through the peace, quiet and insight found in meditation, you could easily be guided by that "still, small voice" toward the psychic tools you are destined to use. We really are all members of a vast and magnificent cosmic orchestra. Find your instrument, join the band, and start making beautiful music.

Busy yourself as much as possible with the study of divine things, not to know them merely, but to do them; and when you close the book, look round you, look within you, to see if your hand can translate into deed something you have learned.
~Moses of Evreux

Dreaming

with Chris Robinson

> *Weary with toil, I haste me to my bed,*
> *The dear repose for limbs with travel tired,*
> *But then begins a journey in my head,*
> *To work my mind when body's work's expired.*
> *~ William Shakespeare*

"One of the main problems I have when I try to understand what life is and what reality is, is caused by the existence of dreams. In dreams everything we know in our waking life and more can exist. We feel, we hear, we see, our dream world can be as convincing a reality as our real world," says Chris Robinson, who is known in England and abroad as "the Dream Detective."

That the real world and the dream world are inter-related is beyond a doubt. It's the precise nature of that relationship that brings up all the questions. Is the land of dreams pure fantasy? Is it merely a dumping ground for the pent up emotions of the day? Is it a means of extra-sensory perception? Is it all of the above? Is it, in its own way, just as real?

The debate will inevitably rage on, but one thing is certain. The dream world can be an effective tool for psychic detecting. For example, in the early '90s, Chris predicted that a certain jewelry store would be robbed. The loss would be £1 million, and he even predicted the date. The events unfolded exactly as he had dreamt them.

Chris has used his psychic talents as an undercover agent for Scotland Yard and the British intelligence services, to help law enforcement agencies around the world, and as a psychic detective with Find Me.

In addition, Chris has proven his precognitive dreaming abilities in scientific studies at such facilities as the Human Energy Systems Laboratory at the University of Arizona.

In "Controlled Experiment Evaluating Precognitive Dreams in a Highly Skilled Subject" submitted to the *Journal of the Society for Psychical Research*, Dr. Gary E. Schwartz states, "The author has spoken with two separate police officials in England who confirm Chris Robinson's longstanding collaboration in law enforcement activities and their satisfaction with his information."

He adds, "CR's overall accuracy was surprisingly high.... The findings provide evidence consistent with CR's claim that he has the ability to obtain precognitive dream information about specific locations."

In other words, and in a very practical sense, careful scientific scrutiny has proven that Chris's dreams can come true.

Detective Sgt. Glenn Clements of the Regional Crime Squad, based in his area, said of Chris, "He is very plausible. We treat everything he sends us with an open mind."

Dreams, dreaming and dreamers

Dreaming is the most common of all paranormal experiences. Everyone dreams, although some don't remember dreaming. Studies have shown that several of our sleeping hours are devoted to the act of dreaming. We even have waking dreams. Our subconscious mind takes over and sends us on amazing journeys through fantasy, fact and startling combinations of fact and fantasy. As long as mankind has been recording information, we have been recording dreams. Those flights of fancy involve the entire range of human experience, including sight, sound, touch, taste, smell and our vast repertoire of emotions.

When we sleep, our brain cycles through a number of rhythms called brain-wave patterns, each of which operates at a different frequency. This cycle is natural, and we all experience the process every time we get a good night's sleep. Dreaming occurs when our brains alter these brain-wave patterns. Changes in our body chemistry, such as the release of hormones, can occur, which may affect the intensity of the dream.

There's a lot going on inside your head when you're asleep: bone growth or loss, muscle and tissue action, nerve activity, blood flow, chemical changes, transmission of electrical impulses, and who knows what else. Somehow, this activity produces dreams, and sometimes the dreamer can put them to good use. As Shakespeare said, "There begins a journey."

With a few exceptions, even the most powerful of our dreams are fleeting things. They aren't usually added to our long-term memory and are quickly lost after we awaken. That's why journaling psychic messages, including dreams, is so important when working on a missing-person or criminal case. Invaluable information can vanish in an instant, never to be retrieved, and perhaps even "the clue" could be lost forever. Pen and paper, electronic notepad, a hand-held voice recorder or whatever is most convenient for note taking should be a permanent element of your psychic arsenal.

Dream language

Chris and other psychics have the ability to see the future in dreams. They are often aware of kidnappings, murders, robberies and other crimes long before those events occur. Time and distance offer no barriers, for the dream world is without limits. A psychic detective in England can sense an event tomorrow, next week or months ahead in his or her home town, in Europe, and across the great seas, and they are often proven by events to be remarkably accurate.

And therein lies the problem.

Sadly, events often have to play out for the accuracy to be proven. How can a dream, an impression or a vision be accurate and at the same time not contain enough information to prevent a tragedy? The answer is basic to psychic work – the paranormal is a world of symbolism.

A dream and a very clear warning about Chris's personal life is a perfect example. He had a powerful dream that he would be struck by lightning in the presence of two large trees – note only two trees were in the dream. Shortly thereafter, he was struck down by a pulmonary embolism that hit both his lungs.

Do you see it?

As he recovered, Chris finally understood the message. He has two lungs. Trees are often called the "lungs" of the earth because they provide the oxygen we need to survive.

Two lungs. Two trees. Being struck down.

Had he given the matter more thought when he first had the dream, perhaps he would have put the clues together. This is a common problem with psychic detecting, and that's not a cop out. By their very nature, dreams are difficult to interpret even when the imagery is crystal clear. For example, let's suppose you have a dream about a man named Jones having a heart attack in a Circle K convenience store. Through the window you can clearly see a sign that reads Maple Avenue. That's pretty specific, but how many men named Jones live in a town with a Maple Avenue and a Circle K store?

Suppose that your dream is more symbolic. It features a child's toy block showing the letters O and K. You hear the song "Casey Jones" or "Me and Mrs. Jones" as a large maple leaf floats over an avenue. The clues are all there. The information is accurate, yet you might have to wait for the event to occur before you can realize just how on-target your dream was.

Dream imagery requires careful evaluation to determine the real meaning prior to the event. Chris once dreamed that the violent Irish Republican Army (IRA) would attempt to bomb two English banks. He had dreamed of two men doing something to mailboxes and the banks. The dream included two empty cups. He interpreted the cups to mean two dead people. Shortly thereafter, two IRA members were killed when their bomb prematurely detonated at one of the banks.

This isn't a problem limited to the world of paranormal investigation. Police and legal authorities face the same difficulties in their more practical environment. Two people looking at the same physical evidence often come up with entirely conflicting conclusions. For every prosecutor bringing a blood spatter expert to court to prove "he done it," a defense attorney brings in his or her own equally expert witness to say "no, he didn't."

Belief, faith, hunches, gut reactions, guesswork and lucky breaks are central elements of all criminal or missing-person investigations, regardless of whether a psychic detective is on the case.

"Working with officers from Her Majesty's Government for more than ten years has taught me that very little of what we see can be termed evidence. It's almost always what we believe, and then we judge the believability of it," says Chris.

The world of psychic prediction is far more complex and difficult than it's shown to be in movies and television. Psychic detectives such as Chris work extremely hard to hone their skills, better understand the world of symbolism, and to "put two and two together" prior to the arrival of four.

Right prediction, wrong town

"I dream like everybody else. It's a mixture of pictures that you can recognize as being reality and pictures that really could not exist."

Perhaps, but Chris certainly puts his dreams to more productive use than most dreamers. His accuracy has been well-documented, but an accurate prediction doesn't always provide enough detail to prevent a crime. That can be true even when the psychic detective gets a lot of clues through a lot of dreams over time. Here's a case in point.

Back in the mid-'90s, Chris began having a series of dreams involving the same or similar images. These included tall buildings, express elevators, concrete boots and meat. Unusual, perhaps, but not too far out for the average person in dreamland. But the repetitive nature of the images, combined with the emotions he felt, convinced Chris that he was getting a message about an upcoming bombing somewhere in England. His belief was confirmed when the dreams began including images of dogs, his personal dream symbol for an attack by the IRA. Something terrible was about to happen.

Again, his problem is common among psychic detectives. You know conclusively that something, usually something specific such as a bombing or a murder, is going to happen, but you lack the specific details to do anything about it. Chris began analyzing his dreams, and he noticed a pattern. Many recurring images began with the letter "M," meat for example. In England, towns have postal codes made up mostly of letters. He wondered. Could the concrete boots from his dreams be symbolic of the letters "CB," the postal code for Cambridge?

The dreams and the clues continued. Chris received a date for the event, a two-hour window in which the bombing would happen, and even the number of casualties. About mid year, he was contacted by another

English psychic who was having similar visions. Not only did she see a terrible bombing, she saw a specific location. Her visions included Piccadilly in London, an area with which she was very familiar. That settled that, or seemed to. The IRA would set off a bomb in Piccadilly in London at the time and date Chris had predicted.

And so it did, sort of. The IRA set off a massive explosion on the predicted date, within the specified time window and in Piccadilly. Observers said that the area resembled photos of bomb-damaged neighborhoods during World War II. Unfortunately, the Piccadilly in question was in the City of Manchester, some 200 miles from London.

That's how the symbolic nature of this ability works. The Piccadilly in London was used because that's an image with which the psychic was familiar. It wasn't a location; it was a symbol of a location. The "M" imagery became obvious, as "M" is the postal code for Manchester.

The message is clear that the psychic detective must examine every bit of information from every possible angle to make sure he or she is getting the right message. It's a most important matter. The message is always 100 percent on target. It's the interpretation that's usually off base.

Anyone wanting to practice psychic dreaming should become intimately familiar with the power of symbolism. A number of books are available in libraries and bookstores that list thousands of images and their commonly understood meaning. Chris emphasizes that the psychic should invest considerable time and energy in developing a list of, and an understanding of, his or her personal symbols.

For example, a bald eagle to one person might symbolize the United States. To another, it could just as easily represent power and nobility, nature, far-sightedness, flight or any of a number of other and equally valid meanings.

Knowing yourself is key to knowing the paranormal.

Chris's technique

Chris's technique is about as basic as you can get, and it's something you're already doing. He dreams. No special rituals or preparations. He writes down any questions about the case he's working on, turns out the light, goes to sleep and dreams. Upon waking, Chris immediately records his dreams in a notebook kept near his bedside. He's conscientious about these records and keeps them all in a library of notebooks. Before grabbing the phone, logging on to the Internet or dashing down to the local police station, he invests a considerable amount of time thinking about his dreams and analyzing his notes and drawings. He's careful to consider all possible meanings of any given image, word or impression.

This attention to detail and willingness to work a case, as opposed to merely reporting a case, is one of the factors that has made Chris Robinson a valued member not only of Find Me, but of many law enforcement agencies around the globe.

The mightiest works have been accomplished by men who have kept their ability to dream great dreams.
-Walter Bowie

Using the Pendulum

with Jeanette Healey and Dan Baldwin

> *The fairest thing we can experience is the mysterious. It is the fundamental emotion which stands at the cradle of true art and true science.*
> *~ Albert Einstein*

A pendulum is nothing more than a weight tied to a string. It can be very expensive and made of exotic stone or metal. It can be very inexpensive and made from common household materials. If you have a rock, a piece of twine, and the ability to tie a knot, you can construct a pendulum. Someone using a pendulum is "dowsing," sometimes known as "divining." It's an art that has been practiced around the world for thousands of years. Officially it's known as "radeisthesia."

Connecting dots

Dan Baldwin was working a kidnapping, a ten-year-old girl who had just disappeared one pleasant, sunny afternoon. He compiled dozens of pages filled with notes over numerous readings. One of those readings produced a specific first, second and last name for the kidnapper, and for the town in which he lived. After some research, Dan discovered that, although the town was more than a ten-hour drive from the girl's home, the two towns were connected by more than 100 years of friendship, family and organizational ties.

Curiosity got the better of him, and Dan decided to see if his pendulum dowsing was producing accurate results. After all, he'd never heard the man's name. He'd never even heard of the town where the guy lived.

Dan called directory assistance. The name, the specific name, was valid. Later he theorized that because of the ties between the two towns, the (suspected) kidnapper would surely return. Out came the pendulum. After a couple of hours work, Dan's notes reflected a specific date for the man's arrival, the fact that he'd be driving an older-model red truck, and that he'd be staying in a specific motel. Dan called the motel and, using his best "good 'ol boy" accent, asked what time his "good buddy" would be arriving. The desk clerk confirmed that the man was booked for late arrival that Friday.

Again, curiosity won out. On the Saturday morning of the man's arrival, Dan drove to the motel. An older-model red truck was parked in the lot. The stencil of a large Eagle coming in for the kill was on the driver's-side door. Beneath it was the word "predator."

At the encouragement of a number of psychic friends, Dan took all his notes to the detective in charge of the kidnapping. The authorities were polite and seemed willing to accept any information that might help break the case. And then nothing happened.

"Did I do any good at all?" Dan wondered. Worse, "Have I gotten an innocent man in trouble with the law?"

He remained puzzled for several weeks until a nationally known psychic working with the detectives on the case sent word.

"Tell Dan his information connected some major dots."

How does it work?

There are two theories.

One says that the human body can react to the presence of water, petroleum, minerals, electrical currents and even radiation within the earth. The pendulum acts as a device to amplify those sensations so the researcher can recognize them. This is well and good for finding a water well on the old ranch, the next gusher in the oil patch, or the Lost Dutchman Mine, but it doesn't explain finding missing persons, catching the bad guys, or preventing a crime.

Many psychic detectives who use the pendulum believe they connect with a higher power. The pendulum is a convenient and efficient means of communication. Swiss psychologist Carl Jung proposed the existence of a super mind that contains the thoughts of every person who ever existed. Perhaps the detective is merely tapping into this consciousness. Some would say that whatever you want to know can be known, provided you make such connections with the super mind, God, the Goddess, the universe, your higher self, or whatever term your belief system supports.

What's clear is that the successful practitioner uses ideomotor response. That's a fancy way of saying he or she gets a physical response from the subconscious mind. This response can provide answers to questions unanswerable by the conscious mind. Think of your mind as the amount of money you're currently carrying in your wallet or purse. By using the pendulum and by tapping into this higher consciousness, you suddenly have access to all the resources of Fort Knox!

How do you work it?

There are two methods.

One, the practitioner asks questions while holding the pendulum by the end of the string. The pendulum will swing one way or another, each direction signaling an answer. Generally, a swing around to the right means "yes" and a swing around to the left signifies "no." A back-and-forth movement could mean "I don't know" or "Rephrase the question, dummy." (More about this later.) This technique is used to ferret out answers to very specific questions.

Another method is called map dowsing. The psychic detective uses a pendulum in conjunction with a map to locate missing persons, crooks on the lam, lost treasure, precious minerals, petroleum reserves, water or what have you. Some people actually move the pendulum above the map while others use a pointer to touch points on the map. The pendulum responds when you move to or over the correct map coordinate.

The pendulum is a very practical instrument. That's one of the factors that most attracted Find Me member Dan Baldwin to its use.

"It's not magic. It's a tool, a device. It's technology fueled by the mind."

There's no ambiguity in working with the pendulum. Many other kinds of psychic detectives by necessity work with symbols open to many interpretations. Working with the pendulum provides specific answers.

Is the girl missing?

Swing right - yes.

Has she been kidnapped?

Swing left - no.

Is she a runaway?

Swing right - yes.

Is she still in town?

Swing left - no.

The process is time consuming, but the answers to the questions leave no room for misinterpretation. That's not to say the answers are always correct. As with anyone on any job, dowsers have their good days and their bad days. It's also very easy to manipulate a pendulum to create a desired answer. Clarity of mind, focus of purpose, and questions designed for one-word answers are essential for a successful session.

The work is often a process of elimination. Dan was asked to help find a runaway from the Midwest. He began working with his pendulum. Is she headed north? No. West? Yes. Is she on a major interstate? Yes. Is it I-40? Yes. And so on and so on throughout the session. He finally determined (or the super mind informed him) that the missing girl was traveling with a salesman who was headed for Albuquerque, New Mexico, and that he would be staying there for several days.

Using an alphabet chart, he got the man's name. He also divined that the man would be staying at one of two Travel Host motels in that city. Wanting to verify his findings, he called the chosen motel and, using his best southern drawl, asked if his "good 'ol buddy" John Doe had arrived yet. The clerk answered "no," but that the man was scheduled to arrive that evening. The information was forwarded to the local authorities, who promptly checked out the other Travel Host, then apparently dropped the matter.

There's only so much a psychic detective can do.

Choosing a pendulum

You can find two distinct types of pendulums.

One is a simple weight on a string. The other is hollow and is designed to be filled with the substance for which you are dowsing. This substance is called the "witness." The theory is based on the principle of "like attracts like." If you want to strike oil, fill the pendulum with an oil witness. Be wary. Make sure your witness is exactly the type of substance you want. If you fill the pendulum with Three-In-One Oil, that's what your pendulum will be attracted to, not Jed Clampett's "black gold."

The real key to finding a pendulum is to find one that just "feels right" to you. Trust your intuition. You don't have to invest a fortune, nor do you have to have the fanciest pendulum on your block. What feels right to you is what is right for you. Some psychic detectives have pendulums set aside for specific purposes. One might be for missing children. Another might be used strictly to locate missing adults. And still another might be used to track down criminals. Some dowsers have a specific pendulum for use on specific days.

There are no rules. Use your intuition, and you'll find the right pendulum for the work you want to accomplish. Dan has a number of rather heavy pendulums he reserves for outdoors work, where the wind could affect movement of the stone.

How to hold a pendulum

Grasp the string or chain between your thumb and forefinger. Let the pendulum dangle straight down. Some people prefer to loop the string over their forefinger. Try both methods and see which is most comfortable for you. Then ask your questions.

That's it.

Comfort is an important factor. Pendulum work can take a lot of time. Resting your elbow on a desk or table is very effective for combating fatigue. Some people dangle the pendulum over the open palm of their other hand. They believe this helps create more energy. Again, try it out and see what feels right for you.

You'll want to experiment on different pendulums, different materials, and different techniques to discover what works best for you. Chief among your decisions are:

• Using your right or left hand. Some practitioners prefer the left hand because it's "closer to the heart." (Actually, the heart is in the middle of the chest, behind the sternum!) Others just go with their dominant hand.

• Length of chain or string. Work with this. Short or long, you'll find a real difference.

• Type of material.

• Position for holding your pendulum. Whatever position you choose should be comfortable. Pendulum sessions can be lengthy.

• Length of in-depth sessions. We all have a "burn out" point at which we feel the effects of the "law of diminishing return." It's better to take a break than to continue when you're tired, and risk getting inaccurate readings.

Pendulum communication

Making a pendulum move is easy. Just hold it properly and think. Without apparent movement of your hand or fingers, it will automatically begin to move. Think "circle to the right" and, as if by magic, it will begin to circle to the right. Don't force the action. Just let it happen. Circle right. Circle left. Back. Forth. These are the basic movements, and each has meaning.

Set your pendulum

You will want to "set" your pendulum so that the movements are consistent for every session. This is best done by "asking" your pendulum which motion signifies what answer. Of course, you're really asking your subconscious mind for directions, but it helps to focus on the device. Generally a circle to the right is a "yes" answer, a circle to the left means "no," and a back-and-forth motion in either direction is an "I don't know." But be sure to ask this of each pendulum you acquire before you begin work. You're subconscious mind may have a very good reason for giving you different directions. Once you've determined the meaning of your directions, "set" it by stating that "yes" will always be registered by the appropriate swing, and so on.

You can only get an answer to one question at a time. It's impossible to answer a two-part question with a "yes" or a "no." For instance, suppose you ask "Did the runaway girl head out of town on I-40 or I-25?" How can you possibly get a correct "yes" or "no" out of that? You have to ask directions one at a time, which requires an investment of time. The trade off is specificity.

Keep in mind that, despite appearances, there's no magic involved in pendulum communication. The movements are nothing more than ideomotor responses to your neuromuscular system. You may not see or feel your muscles moving, but they are.

As Dan says, "The pendulum is a tool and nothing more. The 'magic,' for lack of a better term, is in our ability to tap into that higher awareness, and that's done with the mind, not the fingertips."

If your pendulum doesn't move, it's perfectly okay to give it a gentle swing to get things moving - provided you don't try to control the movement after that. If you get erratic or jumpy movements, it probably means you're full of energy. Just take a deep breath or two and relax before continuing. Sometimes your pendulum will even run wild on you. Again, you probably just need to reformulate your question or take a couple of deep breaths to relax.

Ease of control can present a real obstacle to getting objective answers. It's incredibly easy to get the answer you want or the answer you think you should get. Just think "yes," and you'll definitely get a "yes" answer. A practitioner can't allow his or her emotions to control the pendulum movement. This can be a real challenge, especially when working on the often heartbreaking cases of missing children. Focus on the question and not on the answer. Allow your subconscious mind to provide the information. Trust the process and trust your gut instinct. Dan will sometime keep his mind focused by repeating the question mentally, over and over, until the answer arrives. Sometimes he tries to keep his mind clear, and other times he simply thinks "truth" over and over.

The pendulum may swing in several directions before settling in on a specific direction, but generally you should get a definite and strong movement within a few seconds.

Be aware that your pendulum can be sensitive to electrical energy. Dan was working on a case when his pendulum went "dead" in the middle of a question. It just stopped moving. Then he noticed all the electrical equipment monitor lights in his office were out. The electricity in his neighborhood had just gone off line.

Question your questions

Think carefully about your question, formulate it so you can get a yes/no answer, then keep your mind focused on the question. If you ask about a missing person, but your mind drifts over to the latest episode of *CSI*, your answers will relate to *CSI*. The subconscious mind can't provide "A" if you're mind is focused on "B." Poorly-worded questions will inevitably produce poor answers.

If the swing movements are slight, you can "ask" your pendulum to swing in wider arcs. It works. Eventually you will develop a definite "feel" for when you are getting the correct answer. You'll just know. Then it's time to move on to another question.

Working a criminal or missing-person case is a step-by-step process. Dan helped track a fugitive hiding in the desert by process of elimination. Using a map of the area where the suspect was believed to be hiding, he slowly closed in on a specific sector.

Is Mr. X in the northern (southern, eastern, western) part of the region?

Is he north of the highway?

Is he east of the river?

Is he west of the north/south running dirt road?

Is he within a mile of the crossroad?

Is he within half a mile of the crossroad? Quarter mile? Fifty feet?

Is he on the south side of the road?

You get the picture. Even though Dan was working a considerable distance from the scene of the chase, distance is not a serious deterrent. You don't have to be on the scene to work on the scene. Even if you're completely lacking in information you can still get accurate details by asking good questions.

Is he on the move?

Is he hiding?

Will he be at this hideout for the next seventy-two hours?

Is he physically healthy? Mentally? Emotionally?

Is he hiding in a structure?

Is it a business structure?

Is it a residence?

Is it one story? Two?

Is the structure brick? Cement? Wood?

Does it have a house number?

Is he alone?

Is there a garage?

Is there a hiding space in the garage?

Is this hiding space below ground?

You see? It's possible to acquire a staggering amount of information if you concentrate, focus and ask the right questions. If you're willing to put in the time and effort, you can get names, dates, addresses, license numbers, and virtually any information you need.
This fugitive was apprehended and is now headed to trial.

Pendulum charts

Pendulum work is slow because you have to ask so many questions. But there are effective shortcuts. You can buy books of charts or you can make your own:

A B C D E G0 1 2 3 4NORTH

G H I J K L5 6 7 8 9WESTEAST

M N O P QSOUTH

R S T U V

W X Y Z

There are a number of pendulum books on the market, and many of them include charts. Dan recommends *The Pendulum Charts* by Dale Olsen. It's a small, spiral-bound book that he uses on every case. He uses primarily the Yes/No, Percentage/Probability, Alphabet/Numerical, and directional charts. Other charts include quantity factors, time factors, health-related charts, automobile diagnostics, relationships, and a host of other concerns.

"Working with charts will significantly reduce the amount of labor in a given session. Instead of asking north followed by south followed by east and then west, you can just ask "where" and let the pendulum point you in the right direction. It's one question instead of four."

Dan's technique

It's important to set aside enough time to conduct a pendulum session. A quiet place where you won't be disturbed is equally important.

Dan isn't very big on rituals. He frequently plays soft music, but that's mainly to drown out the noisy neighbors or kids playing in the streets. He has been known to light candles, but he says that's just because he likes the smell of scented candles. He's big on preparation. He always has his laptop or pen and paper ready for note taking. He works in a well-lit area with enough room for his maps.

Relax

Dan meditates for about twenty minutes before a session, just to still his mind so he can focus on the task at hand. On some occasions, he'll meditate on the missing person or the crime being investigated, but generally he just wants to get centered. Slow and deep breathing, or even self-hypnosis, are good techniques.

Pray in

He utters a silent prayer, "I am one with the Father; the Father and I are one. All is one."

He considers this an essential step. A simple prayer is all that's needed. Those without a specific religious belief can address the universe.

"Infinite. please let my work be for the greatest good."

If you lack religious convictions, ask your subconscious mind to help you work for the greatest good. Dan has even been known to utter the "Shepherd's Prayer," named after astronaut Alan Shepherd. As he was about to be blasted into space on America's first manned rocket launch, he uttered, "Oh, Lord, please don't let me screw up."

"Remember, when you're using the pendulum, you're part of a team effort," says Dan.

Self protection

Psychic detecting can attract negative forces. Depending upon your spiritual or religious beliefs, or lack thereof, you'll have different names for such forces. Whether you believe them to be real or merely negative creations of the mind, they still must be dealt with. (Even people who don't believe in ghosts find themselves whistling when walking by a graveyard, right?)

Again, prayer is a wonderful tool for those who believe in it. Visualization is another powerful weapon. Dan visualizes himself surrounded by a sphere of pure white light. The image should be something meaningful to the practitioner. If you'd rather be surrounded by a battleship, an F-22 Raptor, a team of angels or the U.S. Marines, then by all means visualize that image. Employ whatever rituals you believe make you safe and secure. Knock on wood. Grab that rabbit's foot. Put on your lucky sneakers. Whatever helps you concentrate during your session helps you find that missing person.

Jeanette's technique

Jeanette Healey believes that psychic protection is very important, especially for the beginner. A technique she highly recommends is to visualize that you're putting on a cloak. You can visualize different colors for different moods when doing this.

"Then just ask 'Please protect me against any evil. I thank thee,'" she says. "Then get on with your meditation, clairvoyance or whatever the spiritual work you are embarking on."

• Free your subconscious. The subconscious mind follows orders very well, even non-verbalized orders, even orders you might not recognize you're giving. It's like the GIGO rule of computer operation: "Garbage In, Garbage Out." The quality of the end product, your report, depends on the quality of the original input. There can be a very real conflict between your conscious and your subconscious.

For example, let's say you're working a case involving a missing little girl. Your conscious mind wants desperately for her to be found safe and unharmed. When you engage the subconscious, you may get just the answer you're looking for because that's the order you've silently given. That's the program you've input into the computer. You must be neutral. Make a verbal or mental statement freeing up your subconscious mind so it can give you accurate answers.

"I free my subconscious mind to answer my questions fully and honestly." You can make up your own statement, but you get the picture. The best thing you can do for that missing little girl is to get at the truth, not a hoped-for outcome, but the truth.

• Set your intention. Think about the case you're working on and what you want to learn about that case in the upcoming session. A clear focus helps you formulate good questions.

• Can I? May I? Should I? Initially, always ask these questions about the case at hand. Chances are the answers will always be "yes," but it's best to be certain. Privacy issues could be involved. A criminal or a situation may present a physical danger to you. Your talents may be better used on another case or in another area. There could be any number of reasons for not working on a particular case or a particular case at that moment.

Ask the questions and act according to the answers. As you progress and build confidence in the process and your own abilities, you probably won't have to ask these questions. You'll just know.

• Assume nothing. Dan calls this part of the process "asking the question that comes before the first question." Let's say that you've been asked to help find a man who's been missing for some time. It's a natural first question to ask, "Is he alive?" Your answer is an unqualified "yes," but that afternoon you learn that they've found his body and that he's been dead for weeks.

What happened?

"Most of us believe in life after death. The subconscious mind knows this and supplies the obvious answer. Of course he's alive! He's just gone to glory or wherever we're slated to go when we cross over," says Dan. "You get an honest answer, but one that's misleading because the question was flawed."

The question should have been, "Is he physically alive?" Or, "Has he crossed over?" Our personal belief system will have an enormous impact on our sessions and must be taken into account.

• Ask your questions. Take careful notes. Reformulate questions as you need to. Ask the same question in different ways. Add new questions as new information flows in.

• Follow the information. You have to trust the process and your own instincts. Go wherever the information takes you, regardless of how inaccurate, off base or even crazy it may seem at the moment. Record everything. Something that appears downright crazy to you may make a whole lot of sense to an investigator on the ground.

• Monitor yourself. Make sure you're not pushing your limits and can maintain focus. If you get tired, take a break.

• Verify your accuracy. Do this throughout your session. You can ask, "Is that the correct answer?" Or you can use a percentage/probability chart. If you get consistently wrong or low probability answers, something is wrong. Perhaps your questions aren't focused. Maybe you're tired. Maybe you've done all you can do for the day. Dan will often conduct three sessions before filing a report with Find Me.

Map dowsing

Some psychic detectives work best when they can visit the actual scene of a crime or the place from which someone disappeared. Sometimes that's just not possible. Map dowsing can be used on the scene or it can be just as effective thousands of miles away. Distance is not a limiting factor.

There are two basic methods. One, swing your pendulum gently over a map of the target area. It should begin a "yes" movement when approaching the person, place or thing you want to find. The other method is to move a pointer over different places on the map. The "yes" response will tell you when you're at the right place. You can also use a ruler or straightedge to dowse an east/west line and then a north/south line. Your target will be at the place represented by the intersection of the two lines on your map.

"X" really does mark the spot!

You can even create your own maps if none is available. They may be crude, but they may also be effective. Start with the basics. Is there a river nearby? Does it run north/south? Is there a highway? What is its number? Does it run east/west? Does the highway cross the river? Is there a major land feature nearby? You'd be surprised at how accurate you can get if you just ask enough good questions.

Jeanette combined her talents in psychometry with her ability to use the pendulum for map dowsing to bring closure to a missing-person case.

(Jeanette's background is detailed in Chapter Two.) It was an unusual case. She received a phone call from Martin, the brother of a friend. Someone he knew had gone missing on a brief excursion to Spain. To make matters worse, the missing man, Barry, was learning-disabled. He was in his thirties, but had the mind of a five year-old. A group from his care facility was taken on a holiday. The staff members who accompanied the group lost touch with Barry for just a second, but that was all he needed to disappear.

Barry's family was skeptical, especially his brother, but they were also frantic with worry. Jeanette's guide, Jack, provided some specific information about Barry's brother that helped remove some of that skepticism.

She spoke to the brother. "Don't forget to take your driving license with you to Spain. You forgot it when you visited the USA, and you couldn't hire a car to get around in."

He was astounded. "How on Earth did you know that?" he asked.

"How do you think I know?" she replied. "Spirit."

Jeanette was shown a dark leather jacket with the face of a cowboy on the back.

"I felt straight away that he was dead, but I didn't say this for obvious reasons," she says. She also felt clearly that the caregivers in charge of the trip had been careless. She said nothing about that at the moment.

"Sometimes it's best to keep some things to yourself to avoid 'opening a can of worms.' After the case is closed, some of it can always be reported."

After the meeting, she went home and grabbed maps of Spain. Inch by inch, she began covering territory. When she reached the area of Seville, her crystal pendulum began spinning "fast and furiously." She told Barry's family that they should tell the police to go to a monastery in the mountains outside Seville.

Barry's brother, sisters and their partners made the journey to Spain and they were able to locate the monastery Jeanette had mentioned. They discovered a poem about death and saying goodbye. It had been written by a monk many years before, but they understood it as a message from Barry. It was his way of saying goodbye. Two weeks later, his body was discovered in town, just as Jeanette had seen and dowsed it.

"As a psychic, I know that you're not always called upon to be the one to find people or be the one who can solve every case. I felt so happy at what I had been able to do for Barry," she says.

Map dowsing is not as easy at it may first seem. A pendulum swinging over a U.S. map would be covering hundreds of miles. If you were working with a state or highway map, your swing could still cover dozens of miles. Large maps are fine for getting the general picture, such as locating a basic search area. For detailed map dowsing, you will need a topological map that covers a much smaller area, usually seven to fifteen square miles. These maps show prominent land features, roads, back roads, structures, fence lines, railroads, pipelines, mines, abandoned sites, wells, and other features that are extremely helpful. They are available in your nearest map store, probably in your local library, and can be accessed online.

Even if you're working with a detailed "topo," you will have to work hard to narrow down your search area.

"I encourage anyone who wants to start map dowsing to do some actual field work, even if it's just practice. Get out there, tramp around the bush, brush, briars and boulders and see what kind of labor your work will be putting some poor search-and-rescue person through," says Dan.

A mile-wide by five-mile grid is a small search area compared with all the possible locations in the State of Arizona.

"Small is a relative term," says Dan. The technique is now a standard part of his work for Find Me.

The pendulum is a very practical device, a tool and nothing more. Yet it allows the psychic detective to tap into a higher power, participate in the paranormal and, as Einstein said, experience the mysterious.

Believe nothing, O monk, merely because you have been told it.... But believe what, after due examination and analysis, you find conductive to the ...welfare of all beings.

-Gautama the Buddha

Remote Viewing

with Mary Elizabeth

> *In nature's infinite book of secrecy a little I can read.*
> *~ William Shakespeare*

From *The Arizona Daily Star*: "A hiker missing since Monday was found alive today, six miles off-trail in the Lemmon Creek area of Mount Lemmon, authorities said."

As you might suspect, sometimes the news media doesn't have the full story. From our perspective, the story begins with a call from a member of Find Me to Mary Elizabeth.

"Mary, we've got a hiker lost for four to five days, do you think she's alive?"

Mary says that when she gets a statement like, she goes completely "flat-line" to allow information to start flowing in. She asked the person on the other end of the line to keep talking. Images began to form on Mary's mental TV screen.

"Oh, she's alive alright," she said.

More images appeared. Mary saw a wooded area and a trail head with three separate trails. In the foreground was a sedan-type vehicle and a middle-aged female with a backpack. The description matched information provided by the search-and-rescue team.

The images kept coming, and not all of them made a great deal of sense.

"The next scene on the screen was a pie. Just a pie," says Mary. She hadn't a clue as to its meaning.

"Oh, there's a pie shop nearby, and the hiker visits there whenever she hikes," said her friend.

Mary next viewed a scene of the hiker starting up a specific trail, changing her mind, leaving the trail and veering off and up another trail to the right. The next scene was a flash of a mine shaft. This particular image illustrates that remote viewing images can have symbolic meanings.

Mary says, "I knew this woman was not in a mine shaft, that the image was symbolic. I knew she had fallen into a deep place in a heavily wooded area where she couldn't get out or be seen. She had also injured her leg."

Mary also knew that time was running out.

"She has about twenty-four hours left and must be found, or it may be too late," she reported.

Mary decided to try to get a remote aerial viewing of the scene. She saw the same heavily wooded area, plus some type of construction site with a portable toilet. All this information was passed along to the search-and-rescue team.

The next day, as reported in the news media, the hiker was found alive precisely where Mary and some of the other psychics had seen her.

Defining remote viewing

Joseph McMoneagle, a remote-viewing expert and the author of *Remote Viewing Secrets*, defines the process as "the ability to access and provide accurate information through psychic means, about a person, place, object, or event, that is inaccessible through any normally accepted means, regardless of distance, shielding, or time."

The term "remote viewing" was created by researchers at Stanford Research Institute-International (SRI) in the 1970s because they wanted to avoid any occult or "out there" impressions about the subject of their research. It's been a matter of intense study by the scientific community, military intelligence and the Central Intelligence Agency.

Many details of these studies and experiments are still classified, but it's known that the CIA requested SRI to research the matter as early as 1975. The project was called SCANATE for Scan by Coordinates. The Army Intelligence and Security Command became interested, and in 1978 began a program of study called GRILLFLAME. The program later became known as project CENTERLANE, STARBURST and finally STARGATE, which has received considerable attention in the media and has been the subject of a number of books. The CIA and the American Institutes for Research released some data just before the end of STARGATE in 1995.

How effective was the program? Did remote viewing work? Is it real? You'll get conflicting answers. Government officials tend to downplay any successes of the program. Participants, some of whom have written books on the subject, say just the opposite, and they boast of startling successes. If you're really interested in this form of psychical research, perhaps the best way to find the answer is to find out for yourself. A few guidelines will be presented in this chapter.

Pieces of a fractured puzzle

The psychic detective must learn to trust his or her intuition. Rarely does a single psychic detective receive the complete picture of an event. Information comes in fractured, in bits and pieces, and is often of a symbolic nature.

A remote viewer might see a large capital letter "A" with concave sides. Could that symbolize the Eiffel Tower? An A-frame home? An A-bomb? Could it stand for the word "anarchy" or your cousin Algernon? The viewer has to attempt to understand the meaning of a puzzle using only a limited number of pieces. This is the real value of groups such as Find Me. Different psychic detectives using different methods are able to collect far more pieces of the puzzle than any single investigator.

Even then the group may not have a complete picture. Working closely and openly with law enforcement is essential if anyone is to make sense of all the clues. That simple clue, the letter "A," may have real significance to the authorities who are working with considerably more information. Perhaps they're staking out an apartment building where they suspect a kidnapped child is being held, but they don't know if the victim is in Apartment A, B, C, D, or E. If the psychic detective self-censored that clue because it didn't make any sense, he or she would be withholding valuable information.

As a remote viewer working on your own, it's difficult if not impossible to get confirmation on your sightings. A group effort can provide that confirmation. It can also help you refine the meaning behind your images.

Getting feedback on criminal cases is difficult. And who can blame the authorities? John Q. Public may not understand psychic detecting. He might even reflect that misunderstanding at the next election for sheriff, judge or for team leader of the local mountain rescue squad. Imagine how difficult it is getting feedback from officials who are (1) very concerned with case and departmental security, (2) naturally oriented toward secrecy and keeping "cards close to the vest," and (3) not wanting the taxpaying voters to know that they're operating on information from people who see visions, speak with spirits, and take out-of-body journeys. Unfortunately, the information psychics provide on many cases rarely gets a lot of feedback. Of course, regardless of the amount of response, the work is important and must go on.

Remember everything you see or experience! Record it. Report it. Only then should you or anyone evaluate it.

Effective uses of remote viewing

If these images are so fleeting or so subjective, what good are they? That's an excellent question. Unfortunately, this is where the image of psychics as portrayed in film and television has really skewed reality. Psychic detectives do get only pieces of the puzzle, but those pieces add up, especially when a lot of detectives are on the job.

For example, one remote viewer might get just an image of a rotating letter "O." Another might pick up a couple sitting on a bench seat, eating cotton candy. Another might see a clown dancing to hurdy-gurdy music. Nonsense. But to a detective who suspects an operator of one of a dozen carnival rides of kidnapping, it might make a lot of sense. Clown. Music. Cotton candy. Carnival. Carnival ride with a bench-type seat. Bingo! Ferris wheel.

That's not evidence admissible in court, but all of a sudden the detective on the case can direct his or her efforts toward one individual instead of all twelve.

Author McMoneagle recommends five areas in which remote viewing is particularly useful.

1. Describing real people, places, things, and events. If something is real, it can at some point be checked and verified. False leads or misinterpreted information can be weeded out, and solid information confirmed and refined to perhaps lead to even more clues.

2. **Producing new leads**. While McMoneagle notes that remote viewing shouldn't be used as a stand-alone means of gathering data, it's an effective tool for targeting other sources and technologies.

3. **Reconstructing events**. Remote viewing often can "connect the dots" when law enforcement or search and rescue teams have a lot of information but can't put it all together. Not only can you help make some sense of what information exists, you might also be able to point out where to find some of the missing data needed to complete the picture.

4. **Making decisions**. It's a particularly effective technique for deciding between one of two options: yes/no, up/down, go/no-go, buy/sell, and so on.

5. **Making projections**. Predicting the future is a tricky business. Every action anyone takes, from the second the prediction is made, can

effectively alter the future. Provided the projections of future events are descriptive, they can provide significant and accurate detail. McMoneagle notes that remote viewing is not particularly good at the timing of future events. Still, some refinement could be possible by asking the right questions. Are the people you're viewing in summer or winter clothing? Is the event taking place in the daytime or at night? Is there a calendar in view?

McMoneagle notes that remote viewing is not a very useful tool in some areas. These include seeing a series of numbers, specific words or statements; providing information on mythical or hypothetical events or entities, such as unicorns or UFOs; and producing a specific location. That last one tends to go against public belief, but it's one of the least productive uses of the technique unless there's something unique about the location that clearly identifies it.

Take the Ferris wheel as an example. How many of these are there in the world? Again, we see the value of working with other psychic detectives and the appropriate authorities. The police may have already targeted a specific carnival. Instead of hoping that the police will confirm the remote viewer's information, he or she may be confirming theirs!

Anyone wanting to develop remote-viewing capabilities should practice regularly, to expand the range of capabilities, and to get involved with other people of like mind. It's helpful to join a group, such as Find Me, so that you can receive positive feedback, encouragement, and support from like-minded individuals. We are all much more powerful and can do so much more good when we combine our energies.

Mary's story

Mary Elizabeth's interest in Find Me follows a natural progression of her interest in children and their welfare. She is a child-protection caseworker in Colorado.

Mary discovered her psychic abilities as early as age six, through the medium of sports. "I loved sports and, in retrospect, my 'edge' was responsible more than once for anticipating a specific play on my opponent's part," she says.

Her ability to have and to recognize premonitions seemed, at the time, just part of growing up. "I still didn't think I was different." Her skills and abilities continued developing.

"My psychic senses progressed over the years from precognitive flashes to strong telepathic thoughts. I recall having ultra-sensitive hands that seemed to always tingle, and a strong urge to heal. The process of remote viewing arrived without warning."

In 1988, while living in Ohio, she met a medium who insisted she acquire a copy of *Hands of Light* by Barbara Brennen.

"You'll need it some day," said the medium.

Mary bought it, placed it on a shelf, and forgot about it. In 1993, Mary faced personal loss and was dealing with grief when she noticed the book. She opened it and let the pages randomly flip. When they stopped, she read the words "Be still, and know that I am God." This was her personal mantra. "I have a strong faith in God. I but do not consider myself a religious person, but I saw the "Light," so to speak."

At that moment, Mary decided to allow Spirit to guide her life. She sought a psychic healing session "to check my accuracy and convince me I wasn't nuts."

Mary was working full time and raising two kids, yet she felt a strong desire to develop her skills and put them to good use.

"I needed a 'guinea pig' who was tight mouthed and conveniently located." She began "experimenting" on her sister, who was experiencing serious back pain.

"Within a few months of the 'viewing,' Mary began to see internal and external blocks as well as other psychic information and feedback. She could see how these images correlated to each other. She began to experience the sensations associated with every level of human body and spirit, including "auras, the colors, the heat, the cold, the layers of 'garbage' people accumulate over a lifetime, filled with hurt, anger and trauma."

"Spirit guided clairvoyantly to the next issue needing attention with that particular person, whether it be emotional, physical or spiritual."

Mary didn't use any particular process to bring out this ability. She simply quieted her mind through meditation before each session.

Seven years passed, and Mary was well into touch-healing and energy work. She no longer thought twice about the flashes and images that appeared while working with people. Without revealing the source of the additional information and guidance, she began to offer additional assistance.

"As I've come to learn, Spirit doesn't give you what you shouldn't share. But diplomacy and tact go a long way in situations where emotions and health issues are at stake."

Zap!

Friends and people in her workplace often approach Mary for a quick "zap" of healing, or for a remote-viewing scan of a particular ache or pain. She's happy to provide this service, and often offers specific advice on how to proceed with healing.

"A responsible healer and sensitive *never* gets involved in the person's current medical treatment, but supplements and aids the healing process by pointing to potential 'blocks,' regardless of the cause."

A friend, Cindy, complained of shoulder pain that just wouldn't go away. "I had always felt that something was holding her back personally, but I couldn't get a grip on it," says Mary. She explained that sometimes a remote-viewing scan for an injury can draw out other issues. If this were the case, she could expect to experience a certain amount of emotional upheaval.

"As I began a general scan of her shoulder, my own body became tense, and I felt trapped. A slow-motion scene began to play out. It was as though a big-screen TV appeared in my view. I saw Cindy being violently thrown into a wall by a male."

Mary was uncomfortable with the situation. She wanted to help Cindy, but was unwilling to pry into her private life.

Very gently, she told Cindy that the injury was the result of violence at some point in her life. Mary further explained that the inability to release that event and come to terms with it had settled in Cindy's shoulder at the injury site. Cindy just stared for a moment, then related how she had been abused in a previous marriage. As Cindy narrated her story, Mary could see the events scene by scene on her mental TV. Mary removed the energy block, and Cindy made a commitment to deal with the pain.

A few weeks later, Cindy told her that whatever Mary did made her cry for days, but once she was done, the pain completely disappeared.

There's a happier ending to this story. A few months later, Cindy and Mary met for lunch.

"I don't see auras, I feel them. Cindy's energy field softened to a gentle pink. Being that tact isn't my strongest trait, I simply asked if she was pregnant."

"No," was the reply.

Cindy had remarried, and she and her husband were hoping for a family, but that would be some day in the future.

"A few weeks later, I ran into Cindy again, and the first thing out of her mouth was, 'How did you know? I'm pregnant! I was a few days along when we had lunch.' She gave birth to a beautiful girl later that year."

Freeing Michael

Mary's involvement in the murder case of a man named Michael happened quite by accident. She was chatting with a friend who mentioned a murder that had occurred in 1994. Mary was not living in the area at the time, and reminded her friend of that fact.

"At that moment, flashes, images of words, clues, whatever they may be were coming to me faster than I could possibly keep track of," she says.

Mary asked her friend to start writing down the information as it poured out over the next twenty minutes. She wasn't shocked in the least. As it turned out, she has precognitive dreams all the time, and Michael was already at work trying to get through to her.

Over the next six months, Michael's spirit was busy, making sure that no one, including the original investigator, got a good night's rest.

"Coincidences were happening all over the place," says Mary. "The murder site, by then a closed business, remained an eerie reminder of a quiet, Colorado winter night when desperate people took the life of a husband and father."

The authorities had plenty of clues, including a description of the suspects and their vehicle. Yet, the murder remained unsolved.

Mary began to meditate on the case and to develop visual images of a man she'd never seen. She knew the location of the murder, and that was about it. She began developing a list of facts about the crime.

"I could 'see' an actual list relating to the victim, crime scene and the perpetrators. As time went by, I became obsessed with Michael and why he couldn't rest. I knew he was trapped here and I needed to know why."

Mary decided to take a chance and come out of the "psychic closet" by approaching a law enforcement officer with her information. To her surprise, he was one of the original investigators on the case. He took her data, but remained cool and cautious. Sure, a lot of Mary's facts matched those of the case, but they still had to be proved accurate. In cold cases, that could take years.

The former owner of the business allowed Mary and her friends access to the building.

"I walked in and, to my complete shock, everything looked as it had in my visions: the old clay tile, the coolers, soda dispensers, and the area where Michael had been killed. As they began "clearing" the building, messages from Michael began coming through. He was desperate for someone to hear what he needed to say.

"The interesting thing is when Spirit and the love of the deceased are combined in an effort to seek forgiveness and send love to the living. Spirit is *never* wrong in the information that's transmitted. If the intentions are sincere on the part of the deceased and the medium involved, healing and resolution can begin.

"The sad part for me was that Michael desperately wanted his daughter to know the truth. I have no way to do that at this time other than telepathically," Mary says.

On the tenth anniversary of Michael's murder, she decided to visit the scene of the crime. That date proved to be a major stepping stone for Mary's development as a remote viewer.

"As I sat in my car, looking into the windows of the gas station, I began to meditate."

The clock indicated that, in two minutes, the anniversary of the murder would arrive.

"I slowly went into a trance-like state, and once again the movie in my head began to play out in surreal slow motion. I watched the killers as they planned, approached and spoke to the victim. I saw what they purchased, witnessed the murder, the getaway and found myself literally inside their vehicle listening to their comments and, yes, laughter. I was sickened."

Mary saw many other facets of this case, which is still open as of this writing.

"There is absolutely no doubt that, in time, this cold-hearted crime will be solved. The hardest thing I've found in this work is the acceptance and patience that all answers come in time – not necessarily in the time frame we would like them answered, but they do come. It's my experience that all involved in any crime, from the perpetrators, to law enforcement, to the bereaved families, to the psychics, all play a part, and are learning specific spiritual and life lessons individually and collectively. When all that occurs, cases are solved."

We are here to help and to be helped

"My belief is that if you're truly here to help others, those in search of physical, spiritual and emotional healing will find their way to you. Similarly, these are the same people who advance our intuitive abilities, and the tables are often turned as to who is healing whom," says Mary. "Toward that end, you naturally gravitate toward the things that will help you develop spiritually and psychically, regardless of your place in the psychic chain."

In other words, if you seek, you will not only find, you will be found by like-minded individuals.

Mary believes that remote viewing, as with other psychic skills, can be developed by anyone.

"It's my belief that we all arrive with the same abilities and make a conscious and spiritual choice to develop those that benefit the needs of others."

To see clearly is poetry, prophecy, and religion – all in one.
-John Ruski

Guides and Angels

with Sunny Dawn Johnston and Amanda Schell

> *I send an angel before thee, to keep thee in the way.*
> *~ Exodus 23:24*

Many members of Find Me work closely with spirit guides and angels. The two are distinct entities, with different origins and somewhat different purposes. Two views of working with angels and guides are presented by Sunny Dawn Johnston and Amanda Schell.

A successful encounter brings closure

One of Sunny's experiences illustrates a common belief among psychics – there are no coincidences. Often what we perceive as chance encounters provide opportunities for psychic encounters, experiences, help in finding missing persons, and closure for grieving individuals and families.

Sunny conducts regular sessions in which the public is invited to ask about the psychic world. One of her "regulars" brought a friend, basically a walk-in, to the session, someone there out of mild curiosity. As the attendees sat in a circle and began asking questions, she noticed the spirit of a tall, handsome man standing between an attendee and her "regular" guests. The man had a beautiful smile, practically beaming.

"Has either of you lost someone?" Sunny asked, providing a brief description.

The guest responded, "I don't know."

Sunny pursued the matter with a few gentle questions, and the woman responded, "Well, that sounds like my brother. He's been missing for a year."

"The whole vibration of the room changed at that moment," says Sunny. "When I see someone in that way, it means he or she has passed on."

She received a number of messages regarding the missing man, which helped bring this woman some closure. More than that, she put her in touch with Find Me.

"After all, twenty or thirty psychics working a case are better than one."

As this book was being written, Find Me is aggressively pursuing this case, all because a troubled woman was a walk-in to a psychic meeting. There are no coincidences.

Angels – everyone's birthright

Many believe that angels are assigned to us at birth. They are present at our births and remain with us throughout our physical lives. They also are present to meet and guide us when it's our time to cross over. They exist before, during and after our physical lives on this planet. Their whole purpose is to guard and guide us throughout our earthly lives.

"My belief is that angels are energy that has never walked the planet," says Sunny. "They are here to provide love, comfort and guidance. They don't intervene, but they do help us on our journey, provided we ask and accept that help."

Spirit guides

Spirit guides are people who have lived on Earth, who have died and have chosen to serve as spiritual advisors to the living. Unlike angels, they act only in an advisory capacity and are not protectors. Spirit guides are always with us, and we may communicate with them whenever we want. Guides often have had the same life experiences or purpose as the individuals they guide.

We may at any time have any number of guides. They come in and out of our lives as needed. Once their service is provided, they can then move on to help others. The time span of an advisory role may be relatively short, or it may last any number of years. They are there as long as we need them.

Often, our guides are deceased loved ones, but not always the ones we might suspect. Guides can be of any race, religion and background. Their advice is always free and given with love. Of course, as humans, we can accept or reject that advice. We still live our lives with the God-given right of free will.

Sunny's story

Sunny grew up in Salt Lake City, Utah. As with many young psychics, she thought very little about her gifts. Her mom was very interested in the metaphysical world, so the subject was a common one around the house.

"We even had a ghost, who introduced me to the workings of 'the other side,'" she says.

Sunny's abilities seemed very normal until she began talking about her experiences with her friends. They just didn't understand about her ability to see angels, spirit guides, ghosts and auras. She didn't have anyone her age with whom to share her experiences. Sunny "learned to keep quiet" so as not to make others uncomfortable.

Many years later, Sunny was with her mother-in-law as she passed away.

"I felt her soul actually move through me as she left, and something in me shifted. I couldn't push away my gifts anymore. That event started me on the path to becoming and owning who I am - a psychic, medium and healer."

Part of that path led to Find Me. Often, when watching television, she'd get visions or have dreams about the news report, story or feature.

The experiences could be challenging. Often, Sunny would have direct contact with murder victims, and actually see the murder as if she were being given a spirit-guided tour of the scene.

"Do I really want to continue experiencing this?" she thought. She realized that the information was divine in origin, and that she had a duty to pursue the cases.

Early on, she was surprised that even the victims of violent or terrible murders aren't really interested in solving the crime, "payback" or even bringing closure to friends and loved ones. They've passed on, and are moving forward on their journeys. Now in a place of unconditional love and acceptance, they often just don't care about their past physical life.

They seem to say, "I'm okay. I'm happy. It's time for you to move on. It's time for you to forgive and heal; I have."

"It can really be frustrating for the families as well as the psychics who work these cases. We're trying to help them find some sort of closure, and all the departed family members want to say is, 'I love you. I'm okay, and all is in divine right order."

Although often meeting with skepticism and resistance from the authorities, Sunny continued her efforts to help. One of her psychic friends suggested that she volunteer her services to Find Me.

"My angels and guides pointed me in this direction. Helping find missing persons and bring closure to families is something I'm supposed to do. They have been preparing me for years. Once I got out of my own way, I could clearly see this was the next step," she says.

My three amigos

No, that's not the name of a motion picture comedy or of a nearby Mexican restaurant. It's the title Amanda Schell has given three of her spirit guides. She says that every human being is assigned a single Master Guide at birth. This guide remains with us throughout life, right through the moment we cross over. Other guides come and go to meet special needs we develop on life's journey. Once those needs are met, the guides step back a bit as they are no longer needed at that time.

"They are here to assist us, teach us and help us spiritually develop if we so choose," she says.

The phrase "if we so choose" is key. We all exercise free will. Your guides will not intervene or interrupt your choice.

"When you begin an open line of communication with your guides and incorporate them into your daily life, you'll find a great joy and sense of camaraderie unlike anything you've ever experienced," says Amanda.

"We should find comfort in the fact that, no matter what situation we find ourselves in, we are never alone. Sound advice and good counsel are always, always available on the spot."

She adds that the more we work with our guides, the more we communicate and trust our guides, the stronger the communication becomes. "This gives a whole new meaning to the term 'teamwork.'"

Believing is seeing

Amanda knew she had three male-energy guides, whom she dubbed "my three amigos," but only one of them ever spoke to her. She referred to him as "the spokesman." He was her master guide. Amanda has a strong visual nature, and she felt a deep desire to see his image. She asked for that image for a full year, but the image never appeared. She finally realized that, in not revealing himself physically, this guide was trying to show her a "bigger picture."

"What I discovered in my quest for a physical image was that by *not* revealing himself to me, he was clearly attempting to demonstrate that the physical here is unimportant."

The guide told her that he could appear physically at any time, but that it was essential that she learn the grander lesson. She discovered that we humans "vibrate" at a certain frequency. The spirit world vibrates also, but at a much higher rate, so fast that there is no need for a physical form as a means of communication.

"As soon as I received this message, loud and clear, I totally let go of my personal need, almost a desperate need, to see my master guide. A day or two later, he revealed himself to me!"

When it comes to missing people, Amanda occasionally receives a message directly from the victim. In most of her cases, this individual just wants to convey that he or she is more than all right, and to please pass this information along to family members.

Amanda can tell the difference between the voice of her master guide and the voices of victims. During one memorable reading, a young woman missing for several years appeared at the end of a meditation.

"I clearly heard her voice, soft and sweet, say to me, 'I'm okay. Don't worry, I'm just fine!' She then relayed to me that she is assisting children on the other side who have suffered a similar fate as she. She also shared with me that she loves to teach and sing on the other side, says Amanda.

Be open to open communication

There are many ways of opening communication with guides and angels, and you should be open to any channels that come your way. Amanda often gets information during her meditations by "automatic writing."

"I have used automatic writing on the computer as well as on a simple pad with pen as a means to gather important information on a case," she says.

Once, while gathering information on a case *via* her computer, Amanda began writing questions about the specific situation. Who? What? Where? When? Why? How? She relaxed and, somewhat to her surprise, she began to tap out the answers on her keyboard. Perhaps "she began" is not exactly correct.

"As soon as I totally relaxed into the question asking, I found that it was not I who was answering the questions on the computer. A matter of fact, it was not my writing at all. Not the style, or manner or word choices. I just completely relaxed and let the energy flow through me, and I was truly amazed at the outcome and at to the specific details that resulted in this session," she says.

Amanda recommends being open to discovering what means of communication best suits you. Follow your instincts as to which vehicle you will experiment with first. Once you have opened yourself and opened your lines of communication with your guides, you will be constantly amazed as to the multiple creative avenues of communication that will be revealed to you. It's truly an amazing journey in personal spiritual evolvement.

Medicine Man

Amanda had another interesting "viewing" of a spirit guide. This was many years ago, during her "dark days" of chronic pain. (See Chapter Seven). She had been encouraged by one of her guides to take up drawing with colored charcoals to facilitate her healing. Although she'd never thought of herself as artistic, she discovered a talent for drawing.

One day, while sketching in her art room, Amanda felt an invisible presence. She asked if it was one of her guides, and received a positive response. A clear, audible voice told her to look to her right.

"As I did, I saw on the wall, directly above a candle-filled wall sconce, an image of a man made by the soot from the candle smoke."

The image was so clear that she nearly fell off her chair.

"I asked for his name, and heard the reply, 'Medicine Man' loud and clear."

Amanda immediately started sketching the image with her charcoals.

"To this day, Medicine Man is a huge part of our family, and he is our family's spiritual advisor."

Sunny's technique

Everyone has his or her own way of conducting a psychic session, and Sunny Johnston has found a number of techniques that work well for her.

1. Work in a quiet space. This can be a special room, with incense, soft music, soft light, or it can be a dark and quiet place. There is no right or wrong way as long as you can get quiet enough to listen. Whatever works best for you is right for you. Quiet is the important factor.

"I prefer to meditate in the bathtub, in nature, or in my own personal healing space." she says.

2. Pray in. Different psychics have widely varying views on divinity, but virtually all doing this type of work begin with a prayer.

"I ask Archangel Michael to surround and protect me so that I don't absorb the energy of the work experience I've been guided to do. As a very sensitive being, I find this is the most important step for me so that I don't take the energy of the people or the situation on."

Archangel Michael is the Angel of protection, and his electric blue energy keeps me safe and secure in all areas of my life."

3. Call in guides and angels. They are there waiting, willing and wanting to help, but have to be invited in. Ask to be a vehicle for Spirit to work through in whatever form is best for the situation at hand.

4. Take a slow, deep and relaxing breath. Allow Spirit to take you where you need to go. Allow all your senses to be "in play." Information may come in through one sense, a combination or all of them.

"It's essential that you ask your guides and angels for help. Ask to be aware of anything that might be of importance," she says. "They don't just jump in. Ask, listen and be willing to follow your gut feeling."

Faith is to believe in what we do not see; and the reward of this faith is to see what we believe."
-St. Augustine

Multi-Disciplinary Approaches

with Nancy Marlowe

Vision is the art of seeing things invisible.
~ Jonathan Swift

Many psychic detectives have and use more than one skill to collect information. That's certainly true of Nancy Marlowe. Her multi-disciplinary approach provides different windows from which to view a crime scene or a missing-person case. Using many disciplines also offers a system of checks and balances because information is gathered in different ways and compiled to create a "complete picture of the crime."

Find Me starts with the basic crime, then fills in as much missing information as possible to develop a clear pattern of what occurred. All pieces of the puzzle are gathered, such as location, weapon, victim identity, suspect identity, vehicles, and so on, formalized in a report, and passed along to the appropriate authority.

A successful multi-disciplinary approach

Nancy's information came in through various disciplines over several sessions, but it was detailed and specific. The man had attended elementary and high school in Wichita, Kansas, and had gone to Wichita University during the 1970s. He was one of four brothers, and he was now married, with two children, and working in the Wichita area in a low- to middle-income occupation.

He'd been in the Air Force and had traveled to Japan, Turkey and Greece. He was active in his church, and he worked with the Boy Scouts. He was a balding white male, of average build, ordinary looking, and between fifty and sixty years old. He could be arrogant. The names Brian, Michael and Simon were in some way associated with him. He used computers, a fact that would aid in his eventual capture. He masturbated near two of his victims, leaving DNA evidence (semen) which also would help authorities.

All this information, and more, was forwarded to Find Me's Kelly Snyder, then passed on to the proper authorities in Kansas. On February 28, 2005, Dennis Lynn Rader was arrested and booked. At trial, he was convicted as a serial killer, one of the worst in the Midwest's history.

Rader was born in 1945, the first of four brothers. He grew up in Wichita, attending Riverview School, Wichita Heights High and Kansas Wesleyan University. He joined the Air Force and traveled to Texas, Alabama, Okinawa, South Korea, Turkey and Greece. The average looking, slightly balding man was active in his Lutheran congregation council and was a former Cub Scout leader. He could on one day be the nicest guy in the world, and on the next an "arrogant SOB."

One of Rader's children was named Brian, an article about the killings had been written by Stephanie Simon of the *Los Angeles Times*, and Rader's pastor was named Michael Clark. Clark turned in a computer disk that aided in Rader's arrest.

Rader sometimes masturbated near his victims, leaving semen at the scene of the crime. DNA records helped identify him as the killer. He was a sadistic murderer who would blind, torture and only then kill his victims, which is why he is known as the infamous "BTK Killer."

Trust but verify

President Ronald Reagan's advice about international treaties applies well to psychic detecting. As previously stated, psychic information generally arrives in bits and pieces and is often in symbolic form. It's easy to get valid data and still misinterpret the information received. A savvy psychic takes a skeptical approach even with his or her own work, always seeking validation through a multi-disciplinary approach. Depending upon the psychic's skill set, he or she may ask guides and angels for tests to confirm the accuracy of the information, swing a pendulum over a percentage chart, throw down Tarot cards or use some other skill to measure accuracy of the information gained.

Trust your instincts, buy verify your results. Someone wanting to join the ranks of psychic detectives should not shun testing. Rather, he or she should embrace challenges. One shouldn't worry so much about being wrong. Focus instead on the times you're right and are able to help someone in trouble.

As one Find Me member says, "Even if you're only ten percent right, that ten percent could lead to finding the missing person."
Remember, baseball's home-run king, Babe Ruth, also led the league in strike outs.

Carrying the mail

Spirits will sometimes communicate with psychics to get them to deliver messages to other humans still physically alive. Why not go directly to the individual involved? Why use an intermediary?

Well, who knows? Perhaps the person who needs to get the message isn't mentally and emotionally prepared to handle a message from the spirit world. How does a spirit communicate with someone who doesn't believe in spirit communication? It could be that the spirits, knowing this, select a living, breathing human to "carry the mail" in the hope that the message will get through.

A remarkable vision

Nancy Marlowe began to suffer lower back pain in her twenties. Seeking relief, she entered a hospital for treatment. One afternoon while enjoying a deep massage in her private room, the phone rang. Her physical therapist took the call, said "okay," excused herself, and hurriedly left.

Nancy closed her eyes and relaxed, enjoying the peace, quiet and comfort brought by deep massage. Suddenly she had a vision of another room in the same hospital. The room was empty except for one woman. Nancy saw the woman collapse and fall face down, dying. Death occurred rapidly, and the body slid slowly across the hard, wooden floor.

At the same instant, Nancy saw this woman's soul emerge from the corpse. The soul appeared as wispy, translucent. It gracefully floated from the woman's body, flowing upward from her feet, up out of the top of the head, much like a butterfly emerging from a cocoon. As the soft, misty soul ascended, a male figure descended from above and took the soul's hand, and the two spirits of translucent light floated peacefully through the ceiling and out of the room. Nancy had observed a remarkable vision of crossing over to the other side.

"I knew that the woman had died, and I also knew deep in my heart that what I had witnessed was perfectly natural, that everything was okay and as it should be," Nancy says. "It was actually very comforting to experience the feeling of calming peace and embracing love surrounding the death, and new birth, of a person's soul. And what a wonderful feeling it was to know we are not alone - ever."

About twenty minutes later, the therapist returned to the room and apologized for the delay. She began working on Nancy's back again. Nancy quietly lay there and wondered if she should say anything about the powerful vision. Although she had witnessed a remarkable sight, she didn't want to be laughed at or criticized, thought of as a "flake," or ever be made fun of again.

Finally, despite her fear, Nancy felt compelled to ask, "Did someone die in the room next door?"

Startled, the confused therapist responded, "Yes. How did you know that?"

As Nancy described what she had seen, the therapist stopped working and stood very still. Her eyes grew large. Visibly shaken, the therapist excitedly told Nancy that the family of the deceased woman was still in the hospital.

Suddenly, the therapist looked Nancy straight in the face and blurted out, "I've got to find them. I'm going to tell them," and before Nancy could say a word, the therapist was out the door.

"Gosh, did that ever scare me," Nancy remembers. "Because I had to just lay there, suspended in time, and hope that I had done the right thing in revealing what I'd seen and knew to be true."

Half an hour crept by, and finally the therapist returned. She had spoken directly to the family and described the woman's soul floating from the body, hand in hand with another figure, a figure felt to be divine.

Nancy's vision had brought this family great relief and comfort. Bringing such peace to families and individuals brings Nancy a sense of accomplishment and purpose as well as a deep peace of her own.

"Peace travels full circle, and we all benefit when we reach out to one another. Today, grieving people can sigh in relief and even laugh at some of the things their loved ones say to them. They know that the people they love are not lost and that they are okay on the other side."

As a medium, she firmly believes that we never die. We simply exist in another form, one we may not see, but one that lives on.

Nancy's story

Nancy is a clairvoyant, claircognizant, clairsentient, medium, profiler, medical intuitive, healer, remote viewer, and empath and telepath She is clearly someone following the multi-disciplinary path. You wouldn't know she has these abilities just by seeing her at the local food mart or shopping mall.

"I am just like you, a regular person with challenges, friends, family and dreams for the future," she says. "I'm not superwoman. I make mistakes. I still sometimes get scared, or don't know what to do. But it's in knowing that I'm not alone and that I do have help that gives me inner strength. We all have this inside of us and must learn to tap into our 'sixth sense' again."

Still, even as a child, she realized that she was somehow different.

"I knew where danger was, or unfriendly people and places I should avoid. It was as if I had a protective radar that could sense ill will," she says.

Nancy could also sense love, dishonesty, and even past and future events. One day, when she was around ten years old, a group of people wanted to take a trip. Nancy didn't want to go because she knew certain unpleasant things were going to happen, and she said so in front of the whole crowd. Little did she know that she was about to be embarrassed beyond belief.

No one there understood what Nancy knew. So, when Nancy expressed her feelings about the trip, the whole grouped laughed and ridiculed her. "How could *you* know what others think or what they're going to do? *Nobody* can do that," they said. And in that moment, with all eyes staring down on her, Nancy wished that she could just disappear.

That night, laying in bed, she finally realized just how different she really was. It wasn't that the other people lacked psychic gifts. They just didn't use them. Nancy was different because she was tapped into her sixth sense and the other side while everyone around her was not.

"This came as a real surprise, that others were not tapping in and using their intuition and natural instincts. I thought other people could see pictures in their minds, hear whispers, see lights from the other side, or just know things the way I did," she says. "How separated and different I always felt as I grew up."

From that day on, Nancy kept her mouth shut about her abilities and didn't express her feelings. She learned to hide who she was. The ridicule was just too painful.

Things change, and in 1997 Nancy's whole world was turned upside down in an instant.

She was involved in a serious automobile accident. She was hit from behind by a large, heavy truck. A ruptured disc was pressed against her spinal cord. Her injuries were so severe that some of the top doctors and surgeons in Houston still don't understand how she is alive today. They don't understand why she can walk, and they can't fathom why she has no pain.

Nancy believes she's well today because she looked forward to being well and whole once again, and she never thought of any other alternative other than complete recovery. It was the power of belief that completely healed her body. She always held the thought in her mind that she WOULD fully heal. Recover she did.

"Thoughts are a form of energy."

Although full recovery took almost a year and a half, Nancy recovered more than just her physical strength.

"I used the recovery time to read, learn and appreciate the miracle I had been given, a new life. I realized it's okay to be yourself and express the voice within you. Because of this terrible accident, I no longer wanted to hide who I was. I wanted to embrace life and the miracle of life we all share. It was then that I found myself and came back home, back to the center of my being, back to the real me. I was once again connected to all that is. It was then that I accepted the power of the invisible."

In 2002, shortly after the Columbia space shuttle disaster, psychic John Edward appeared in Houston. Nancy was one of the 2,500 people in the audience. Conquering her shyness and her old fear, she stood up and addressed the crowd, stating that she had received a message from Rick Husband, the commander of the Columbia. The message was that the crew had not suffered in the explosion. The astronauts also wanted people to know that the space program should continue. They also wanted to thank America and the people of the world for the honor and love expressed at their funerals. They were very grateful and proud to have served, and would do it again.

The message was a "Thank you from the other side." This event is documented in John Edwards's book *Afterlife: Answers from the Other Side*.

Skills

Nancy has learned to tap into quite a few skills, so she uses a multi-disciplinary approach to gathering information. Here, in her own words, is a list of those skills and a description of how she uses them

1. Clairvoyant. I have always seen "things." I get flashes of pictures and see the scene. It can occur in past, present or future time. The pictures appear as a color film blinking on and off, as if one frame is shown, followed by another and then another. I see people and spirits doing things. I see events happening. I see pictures…flash, flash, flash…the pictures appear rapidly, one at a time. If I'm lucky, the 'reel' will run a few moments longer, and I get a full movement scene.

2. Clairaudient. I hear clearly. Most of the time, there's a subtle whisper in my right ear. Other times, it's as if you and I are having a conversation in real time. The voice is as clear as if the spirit, angel or guide is physically in my presence. These messages often come in quickly and complete, even if it's a vast amount of information. However, I'm able to comprehend everything immediately. It's like I've been "downloaded" with information just like you download data onto a computer.

3. Claircognizant. I "just know" about things. For instance, I just know how something works (like a rocket), even though I've never studied aeronautical engineering. I just know what happened somewhere. I just know the answer to a question. I just know something without a doubt. Claircognizance is a very clear, accurate knowing that is seldom wrong.

4. Clairsentient. I sense things. I sense feelings, danger, honesty, dishonesty, depression, joy and love. Clairsentients feel the presence of the energy surrounding a person or situation. I read minds using mental telepathy. I know what people think and feel. It doesn't matter if the person is living or dead. The dead allow me access to their thoughts. Living or dead, people can be located anywhere in the world through the energy of their individual thoughts.

5. Empath. I am empathic and experience someone's pain or happiness. I am in empathy with that person, and I feel the way they feel. In my travels, I don't like visiting places such as former concentration camps, dungeons or execution sites because my empathic feelings draw me into the heaviness, fear, sadness of the event, and these negative feelings stay with me awhile. I don't like the horror or the depression or fear that surrounds certain places. However, the good news is that when I visit a place of love, hope and goodness, I'm pleased to be able to enjoy all the wonderful feelings lingering in that place. They become part of me too. And I relish this.

6. Remote viewing. I can locate someone anywhere in the world and tap into their energy just by knowing his or her name. I can hear them, see them, know what they are thinking (past, present, future), but I cannot find my lost car keys! I use remote viewing to locate missing people.

7. Medium. I'm able to sense the presence of people who have passed over. I see them, hear them, and feel their presence. They talk to me. They appear to me. They leave me messages on my caller ID. They crack mirrors in my house and flicker lights. They interfere with telephones, computers and clocks.
I also see, sense and talk with angels and guides. The spirits, guides and angels sometimes physically "nudge" me in the small of my back to urge me to take action and go forward. They can be very persistent in wanting to be heard, and they will continue to "poke" at me until I respond.

8. Medical intuitive. I'm able to see inside the bodies of people and animals. I can see cancer, inflammation, bone problems, and so on. I can also see, sense and feel emotional problems. I hear the word of the disease or illness such as "cancer, leukemia, ulcer, depression."

9. Healer. I'm able to channel energy to heal. I channel this energy through my hands. I also channel energy across distance with my thoughts and mind. Emotional healings, such as those of anxiety, fear, depression or anger, often are experienced immediately. Physical healings can be immediate or over time.

10. Profiler. I'm able to "read" an individual's thoughts, intentions, deeds, values and personality. This is of help in identifying good employees, criminals, and any relationship areas where information about another person would be helpful. This is helpful for lawsuits, corporations, law enforcement and personal relationships

11. Psychometry. Any object stores information and retains memory. I can "read" these memories by touching the object. I can tell you about the owner of the object and the people around the owner. I can tell you about a battle just by holding a stone from the battleground.

Nancy's technique

Everyone eventually develops his or her own technique for psychic detecting. A good place to begin is to follow in the steps of an experienced hand before venturing out on your own. Here are some of Nancy's basic techniques.

1. Psychometry. To read an object, hold it in your hand and look at it, then feel the texture. Is it smooth or rough? Run your hand or fingers slowly across the surface and begin to receive psychic impressions. These impressions are subtle.

2. Connecting as a psychic, medium, medical intuitive, or remote viewer. Maintaining a healthy body and mind is essential for a strong connection. The stronger a person is physically and mentally, the stronger the connection with the other side. Nancy meditates every day at the same time, taking herself into a trance state where she asks questions and receives answers. The meditation usually takes her deeper than when conducting a reading while not in trance. Since she sometimes receives more detailed information in the trance state, Nancy always meditates before doing a reading and starting her day.

"Meditation helps my day run smoother and with less effort. It also brings a sense of peace, clear direction and well being."

Connection is also boosted with good physical health. Nancy exercises to keep her body functioning better, with a fairly regular routine of exercise. Just being outside on a nice day and being surrounded by the fresh air and sunshine can be beneficial. Oxygen is essential to clear reception and good health.

Eating as sensibly as possible, and still indulging often enough to enjoy delicious foods, keeps life balanced for her.

"Balance emotionally with meditation. Balance physically with exercise and diet. And balance spiritually with prayer," Nancy says.

This lifestyle helps her feel whole and connected with the Universe. Information can be very clear, with direct questions for "yes" or "no" answers. If she wants the answer to a "yes" or "no" question, she just asks for a "yes" or "no." Sometimes a clear, audible "yes" will be heard, and sometimes a feeling or a knowing of "yes" will be sensed.

"Yes" answers are never vague. However, "no" questions can come in either way. The answer will be clear or it will feel muddy, with a vague, not-sure feeling attached to the "no." If you're not sure if the answer is "yes" or "no," then the answer is definitely a "no."

Learning to visualize will increase the amount of knowledge you receive. Visualize and "become the object." Visualize and place yourself at an event. Visualize and become part of an internal organ. Practice visualizing "going into" the core of something such as different metals, an animal, your computer. Ask what it feels like inside, ask the temperature. Ask if there is light. Ask the density. Look for disease in a body or look for structure in a leaf. Try to look, hear, feel, sense, know what it's like inside the thing you are visualizing.

Try practicing by visualizing colors one right after the other in a rapid fashion. Go from red to green to blue quickly, and see the colors change. Visualization helps train your "Third Eye."

The main thing is to just continue practicing. Practice strengthens your gifts.

3. Medium. To call in Spirit, Nancy sometimes touches and/or looks at photographs. She stares at the photo, runs her hand across it and talks to the person with her mind. She asks them to come to her, to appear and to speak. This method of combining psychometry, clairvoyance, clairaudience, clairsentience pulls the spirit close. Another way to draw a spirit in is by focusing on the name of the spirit, then locating its individual energy in the universe.

You can also speak with someone who knew the deceased person, then go in through that person's energy to locate the energy of the dead person. She asks all people requesting a reading to write down all their questions before the reading. Since she is a medium, the information is channeled. No cards or other tools are used.

If records exist, it's often possible to validate a reading. For example, while visiting a friend in Baltimore, Nancy attended a meeting. There, she "saw" a Quaker woman, a ghost who spoke her full name. Intrigued, Nancy searched genealogical records and located the woman. Not only was there documented proof that the woman had lived in the area during the 1600s, she turned out to be an ancestor of Nancy's friend.

When she sees see dead people, she begins to ask them to identify themselves and to show their hair color, size, skin color, clothes and so on. She asks for a conversation with the spirit. When she's trying to find a missing person, she locates the energy of the person and speaks to him or her.

"Show me what it looks like where you are. Tell me what happened to you. Tell me who did this to you. Are you happy? What do you want me to do for you? Ask clear, direct questions of the spirits for a clear answer.

"Most people have a presence always with them, while other people have many, many entities surrounding them. I have seen some people with hundreds of angels fluttering all around them," she says.

These people seem to walk in light and have a glow about them, and other people are drawn to their beacons of goodness and light. Often a person with many angels works in a humanitarian field or is deeply spiritual. They literally "let their light shine."

Nancy recommends reading everything you can on the metaphysical world, talking to other people about their experiences, attending workshops, meditation, learning about "chakras," writing down and keeping a record of information you receive. Learn to be quiet and go within. Meditation is good, as is creativity, being outdoors, beautiful music, exercise, sex: All produce trance-like states that cause you to go within.

Cleansing the energy from a session

Many times, Nancy imagines a white bubble of white light around her or people she loves and wants to protect. You can do this in your car while driving, in your home, on a plane when traveling, and so on.

"However, I live my life knowing that I am being watched over by Spirit at all times. Since I know and understand that all people are from the light and that light destroys darkness, I am not afraid of 'bad' spirits or ghosts or anything evil. I live in the light," says Nancy.

Profiling

Nancy begins by hearing the name of the people being profiled, then begins to locate them in the universe. Before she sees them, she senses their energy. She then gets a sense of how they're feeling emotionally. She also gets a sense of their integrity.

Mental telepathy

Nancy uses mental telepathy and can hear exactly what the profiled individuals say in their heads. She can also hear what they say to other people. It's in asking to hear, see and feel that you get the information.

People often ask if she can read their minds.

"The answer would have to be 'yes,'" she says. "The day will come when we will use mental telepathy to communicate, and that day is closer than we think."

If finding a missing person is like putting together a puzzle, it makes good sense to put as many pieces on the board as possible. A multi-disciplinary approach is a sure way to add those extra pieces. For the skeptical psychic detective, it's also a sound means of putting checks and balances in place, and continually validating your own skills and abilities.

Things don't change. You change your way of looking, that's all.
-Carlos Casteneda

Oracle Card Reading

with Sunny Dawn Johnston

Footprints in the sands of time are not made by sitting down."
~ Anonymous

If you're serious about becoming a psychic detective or just developing your God-given abilities as a psychically gifted person, at some point you have to stop thinking about it and start taking action.

One well known means of getting started is with Oracle or Tarot cards. This is an especially effective tool for those who are visually oriented. You can find all kinds of Tarot cards in all kinds of styles and illustrations. Whatever your interests, there's a deck that matches them. Some are traditional, some feature historical or mythical characters, and some are really "out there" in terms of artwork and design.

As with any type of psychic tool, you should trust your instincts in selecting the deck best suited for your personality. As with the pendulum, meditation, or any other psychic tool, the cards are not magic. They don't posses any power, nor do they confer power, wisdom or information. The power is all within you. The cards just provide a means of accessing information. They are just tools to help you tune into that may be unseen with your physical eyes.

As with any psychic tool, it's essential that the practitioner trust the information that comes through. This acceptance can be especially difficult for the beginner, who lacks the skill and experience of someone who's been at it for some time. You have to let go of your fear of being wrong, and trust that you're getting legitimate information. Then do your best to share that information as clearly as possible without adding your own personal interpretation.

Specific details about the cards and how to use them are included in this chapter. But first, here's a success story that shows how dramatically an Angel card reading can affect human lives.

Innocence is in the cards

Find Me member Sunny Dawn Johnston reads a special deck known as Angel cards.

Sunny was working with a woman who had come in for a reading, a woman with enormous emotional trauma. Sunny spread the cards on her table and immediately knew (there's that "knowing" again) that the woman and her family were in turmoil about her nephew, who had been murdered just the week before. They were experiencing tremendous fear, grief and uncertainty around the remaining family members. They were confused and uncertain about the possible role one of the nephew's friends had played in the murder. It seemed to law enforcement that this friend was an accomplice, and that he actually helped the murderer get away.

"I saw the entire event through my 'spiritual eyes,'" says Sunny. "I knew immediately that the nephew's friend was not guilty. A second friend had actually walked into his home, to his bedroom, and had committed the murder with his three family members in the living room. The first friend had merely encountered the killer just outside the crime scene. Unaware of the just-committed murder, he walked away with the killer. Later, both were arrested and jailed for the killing – one guilty and one completely innocent," Sunny explains.

"My Angel cards were the tool that opened the energy for me to get a direct message from the nephew. He said his death didn't matter. It was his time to leave, but he wanted to let his family know that an innocent man was in jail for his murder."

Sunny shared this information with the family, and they were able to let go of their negative feelings toward the innocent man. In fact, the family approached the police with the information, and asked for his release. At the time of this writing, it's unknown if the innocent man has been released.

The Tarot deck

Each Tarot deck consists of seventy-eight cards divided into two main sections. The twenty-two cards of the Major Arcana represent the greater or more powerful events in life. The fifty-six cards of the Minor Arcana represent more of the day-to-day matters we face. The Minor Arcana is divided into four suits: wands, cups, swords and pentacles. Each suit has fourteen cards, one (or Ace), numbers two to ten, Page, Knight, Queen and King.

How the deck actually works is something of a mystery. It's generally accepted that information is available for those seeking it. Those who choose to tap into this resource can gain a remarkable amount of insight, information and guidance. The cards are merely a tool we use to gather information.

Reading the Tarot deck

To tap into this vast resource, the Tarot reader places a number of cards in one of many patterns. These patterns are called spreads, the most common being the Celtic Cross spread. It's a good spread to begin with. Of course, you can use only one card, three cards, or any of the other spreads. It's a good idea to experiment with different spreads so you can find the one or ones that suit you best.

Let Spirit guide you. Your personal instincts and insights should always take precedence over interpretations from a book. After all, you're much closer to the case or the crime than the author of a book. Again, don't allow self doubt to cloud your reading. Chances are you're much more accurate than you might believe. Again, trust the process and trust yourself. Read the cards and record whatever you experience. You'll be surprised at the accuracy of your work.

Begin by formulating a question. Give the matter some thought so that your work with the cards will be focused and on target. Unlike the pendulum, in which you must ask specific and highly-targeted questions, you can be very general with the cards. In fact, you'll want your questions in some cases to be general so as to avoid cutting off areas you might need to explore.

With pendulum work, you would need to ask, "Is it up or down?" When working with the cards, you could just ask, "What's going on?"

Once the question is formed, ask it and then start laying out the cards in the spread you've chosen. The cards will provide information relating to the question.

For instance, if you drew the eleven card (Justice) from the Major Arcana, the card is telling you, "Someone has investigated the situation concerned and has arrived at a decision that is fair and honest." But, as they say on the game shows, "there's more." If you pull that card, but it's upside down or "reversed," the meaning changes to "Injustice and possible loss. Someone feels inadequate and is unable to change the situation."

These meanings are found in any number of guidebooks to reading Tarot cards. They provide valuable information, but those answers don't provide all the information available to you.

Actually, there are two meanings for every card you lay down. First, there's the meaning from your guidebook or text. Then there's a second and the more important, more powerful meaning. That's the meaning inside your head. This is perhaps the single most important lesson found in this chapter.

Look at every image on the cards you pull. If a pile of seashells gives you the impression of a pile of coins, then a pile of coins is the message from that card that day during that reading. If you look at a castle on a card, but get the impression of a toy store in the nearest shopping mall, then that's your message. If the spires on the castle look like missiles ready for launching, that's the message. If the castle gives you the impression of a wedding cake, then that's your clue. That's where you would start looking for that missing person.

The messages from the cards change every time you look at them. Ask yourself, "What is this card telling me right now?" Then trust your instincts and accept the message that comes through.

The Celtic Cross spread

As previously noted, there are any number of good spreads you can use. This one is presented to show you how the process works. First, shuffle the cards while thinking your question. First we'll note the positioning of the cards, then we'll get into the meanings of those positions.

Place the first card down. The number two and three cards are then placed vertically above the number one card. Place card number four to the immediate left of the number two card. Place the number five card across and on top of the number two card, and the number six card to its immediate right. This forms a basic cross. Place the number eight card below and to the right of the cross. Then place cards eight, nine and ten vertically above it. That's the complete pattern of the Celtic Cross.

What does it all mean?

Card #1: This is the basis of the matter at hand.

Card #2: This represents where you are at the moment.

Card #3: These are your hopes and fears about the situation.

Card #4: This symbolizes the past and what is passing now. Although the matter may be passing, it can still affect you.

Card #5: These are the forces for or against you. If the card is positive, then the forces are with you. If negative, the forces are against you.

Card #6: Represents the near future.

Card #7: Reveals how the near future will present itself to you.

Card #8: Indicates new developments or the effects others could have on you.

Card #9: Shows you in the environment of the future.

Card #10: Indicates the final outcome.

This topic is much too complex to explore in any detail here. Your local bookstore and library will most certainly have detailed, in-depth materials to help your study.

Please remember that there are a number of ways to read any given card. There's the "book" meaning, including the reverse-key interpretation. Then there's the personal meaning you give to the card each time you conduct a reading. Although the textbook meanings are important and provide sound guidance, your personal interpretation is far more significant than the meaning found in any book.

Sunny's technique

Sunny advises to remember that the cards are just tools. They're just paper and ink. All the power is within the reader. Her procedure is pretty basic. It's also quite effective for her, her clients, her students and the people who come to Find Me.

1. Pray in. Set an intention to be an open channel of healing and love. Call in your angels and guides, and ask for their help and guidance. Sunny also calls in the Archangel Michael for extra protection against negative energies.

2. Shuffle the cards. Sunny shuffles until the "feeling" is right.

3. Lay out the cards. In Sunny's case, she goes strictly by intuition and follows the guidance provided at each reading by her angels and guides. Sunny asks her guides how many cards her client should pick (if no client is present, how many she herself should pick for the situation at hand).

4. Allow the client to flip the cards. Allow the information to come through. Sunny advises to pay very close attention to all your senses...how you feel, what you see, what you hear, the thoughts that pop into your head...even what you smell. All these senses work together to give us a clear picture from the spirit world.

Care for your card

It's important to "clear" your cards. You can do that with a prayer, asking your angels and guides to clear any energy that's not for the highest good. Or you can use a clear quartz crystal, setting it in sunlight or moonlight for twelve hours or so, then putting it atop your cards to release any unwanted energies.

As with any valuable tool, you should take good care of your Tarot cards. Here are a number of steps for the care and protection of your cards. Keep them in a wooden box, a cloth bag, or wrap them in fabric, preferably silk. Keep them away from prying eyes and curious people. These are your cards. They're not toys and should not be handled by those who don't respect or know how to use them.

One-on-one readings are the exceptions. In these cases, you'll want your subject to use his or her energy through the cards. In most cases, you'll want the other person to shuffle and cut the cards for you.

Practice, practice, practice!

Study your cards every day. What images come to mind? Do you see mountains? Colors? Lakes? States? People? Animals? Astrological signs? Get used to seeing images within the images printed on the cards. This is how your higher self sends you messages. Are those seashells a pile of coins?

Be sure to always use a cover for the table or surface on which you place your cards.

If you're seriously interested in becoming a psychic detective or in just enhancing your abilities, Tarot card reading is a great place to start. Why not start today? Stop sitting in the "sand" of your wishes, stand up, and start making some footprints. You might make a lasting impression on someone's life.

All that Adam had, all that Caesar could, you have and can do.... Build, therefore, your own world.

-Ralph Waldo Emerson

Channeling

with Nancy Marlowe

We are not human beings having a spiritual experience. We are spiritual beings having a human experience.
~ Pierre Teilhard de Chardin

Sanaya Roman and Duane Packer, authors of *Opening to Channel*, describe channeling "as a powerful means of spiritual unfoldment and conscious transformation. With channeling you can access all the ideas, knowledge, and wisdom that is and ever will be known."

They state, "As you channel you build a bridge to the higher realms. You access these higher realms by connecting with a high-level guide or your higher self."

Channeling is a relatively new term for a very old technique of acquiring information unavailable here in the "real world." Of course, most psychics would argue that all psychic activity takes place in the real world; it's just that some parts of that world are less accessible and more complex to explore.

Channeling is a way of communicating directly with spiritual beings who are not incarnate. The channeler allows a spirit to inhabit his or her body for a period of time. Questions are asked, and the spirit provides the answers using the body and vocal cords of the channeler. Although there are cases of involuntary channeling, generally this process requires the permission and active participation of a volunteer, the channeler.

Channeling works well for psychic detecting. For example, Nancy used the technique to help locate a missing man in North Carolina. Among the facts she channeled were: The man suffered head trauma, he was in a wooded area near water, and he would be found off a specific highway. Later, the authorities searching a section of that highway found the man's body. His vehicle had left the road, striking a tree that had caused severe head trauma. The area was heavily wooded and near a pond.

The technique is probably as old as humankind and has been used in various forms throughout recorded history. The oracles of the Greco-Roman world, such as the famous Oracle of Delphi, were probably channeling spirits. The mystics and prophets of the ancient Middle East who heard voices or who sometimes entered a trance and spoke with voices not their own were certainly channeling. Some, if not all, shamans, witch doctors, healers and mystics of all cultures from all ages practiced the art.

Channeling channels

There are different levels of channeling. Different channelers will have somewhat differing opinions and definitions, but these altered states generally fall into one of three categories.

In a conscious channel, the channeler feels that he or she is completely wide awake and aware of all that's happening in the immediate environment. Observers may not notice any changes in the channeler's body language or tone of voice.

In an altered-state conscious channel, the channeler may feel fully aware of the physical environment only to realize later that he or she can't fully remember the information passed through. It's something like trying to remember a vivid dream only to get flashes of it when fully awake.

During a trance channel, the channeler "goes away" and the channeled entity takes control. This control can be light to heavy. In a light trance, the information may be communicated telepathically. In a heavy trance, the entity takes full control of the channeler's body to better convey the information. Some describe the experience as a "full body massage" channel. Remember that this giving up control of part or all of one's body is a voluntary act.

Which type is best? Well, which is the best way to tie your shoes? Left foot first or right foot first? What's the best road to take on your vacation? What's the best flavor of ice cream?

The answer is, of course, "That depends."

The best method of channeling for you is the one in which you're most comfortable and most accurate. That being said, once you open yourself up to channeling, the spirit may have other ideas. These are important matters to consider, especially for people who have control issues.

Channeling isn't a "takeover"

Fortunately, the Universe operates by a set of rules. We've noted that channeling is a voluntary act. Many of the reported involuntary channelings were probably completely voluntary because the channeler had willingly opened himself or herself to the process. It's something like a person who has been hypnotized by a stage hypnotist into acting like a chicken, claiming to have done so against his or her will. That's just not so. The simple act of agreeing to step on that stage gave the entertainer permission to conduct the hypnotism. No matter what that person said about the experience, his or her actions offered a clear "okay" to the hypnotist.

As in hypnosis, channeling won't cause you to cross your moral line or to do something against your will. Spirits know the rules. If you don't like the information being given, if you don't like the spirit, or if you don't want to continue the experience for any reason, you just ask the spirit to leave.

The law of attraction

"Like attracts like" is a basic rule of the human condition. It's also a fundamental rule of the universe. "Birds of a feather flock together." That's certainly true in the realm of channeling. Generally, channelers attracts spirits who are on the same spiritual and moral plane as themselves. For example, a channeler who is not ethical will attract unethical spirits. And, yes, there are less evolved spirits.

Those channelers who live moral, helpful, open-hearted lives will attract the same type of spirits. That's just the way this thing works. And that leads to another important consideration.

How accurate is channeling?

As if you haven't already guessed, "That depends." And it depends on a number of factors.

Even the most sincere, most talented and most dedicated channelers are still human. That means they bring to the table their own set of moral values, personal experiences, prejudices, likes and dislikes. We're all affected by who we are, where we've been, what we've done, and what we've seen and imagined. The best channelers realize this and make sincere efforts to provide the most accurate information possible.

Again, we're all human. If the channeler has had a fight with the boss, loaded up on too much coffee before the session, just experienced a tragedy, had a bad day or whatever, those events could (emphasize *could*) conduct a less-than-ideal session. The quality of the session greatly depends on the quality of the channeler, and we all have our good and bad days.

Nancy Marlowe points out that when channeling appears to be inaccurate, the problem is usually with the interpretation of the information received rather than the information itself. Her experience with the "BTK Killer" case proves her point. Through Find Me, she conducted a number of channeling sessions, and passed along the information to the authorities. A year later, the killer was arrested. Nancy's information proved to be 80 percent accurate. That's a major "hit" in anybody's book.

Her average would have been higher except for her interpretation of some of the information. For example, although the BTK Killer was married and living with his wife, Nancy got that he was separated and living alone. What happened?

"I don't 'channel paper,' such as marriage licenses or divorce papers. I channel the heart," says Nancy. The killer was living with his wife, but he had no feelings for her. In a very real way, they were "separated," and that's exactly what Nancy picked up. Again, the information was on target, but the interpretation was off. The channeler must be constantly wary of putting his or her "spin" on channeled information.

There's one last, but very important, matter to consider. When we in our four-dimensional world channel spirits, we're communicating with another dimension or perhaps with many dimensions. Communication from that reality may at times be quite difficult to translate into this reality. Try to explain color to a blind person. How do you convey sound to someone who's deaf? How do you express complex ideas to someone who's mentally challenged? Spirits may be experiencing the same challenges in speaking with the human realm.

This is in no way meant to dampen your enthusiasm. On the contrary, you are encouraged to explore channeling if that's your interest and your wish. Just realize that, as with any worthy endeavor, you will face challenges. It's through these challenges that you will grow, expand your psychic abilities and help more people.

Many psychics warn people not to play the expectations game. Unreal expectations, goals or desires can dampen, pollute or even destroy the benefits of a session with a psychic or a psychic group. For example, if you participate in a past-life regression, it's possible that you were Alexander the Great or Joan of Arc, but it's far more likely that you were Alex the plumber or Jeanne the seamstress. The important thing is to experience whatever comes through for you, whether it's a full-blown, 360-degree, sense-u-round experience or merely a bit of an image, a smell, a feeling or an emotion.

The information coming through, however detailed or however fragmentary, is important. Learn to trust.

You don't have to understand the information to use it

One thing Find Me members learn quickly, if they haven't already had the lesson, is to avoid self-censorship. Psychics often only get bits and pieces of a missing-person. One may pick up an image, another may sense a sound or a smell, and another may dowse an address or phone number. One of the founding principles of Find Me is to put as many of the pieces of a puzzle together to create a more complete picture.

Anyone doing this type of work shouldn't hold back any piece of information. It may make absolutely no sense to you, but added to the other bits and pieces, it may be a crucial bit of information.

"Learn to know that the pictures you see, the words you hear, the information you get is real, no matter how little sense they may make to you at the time," says Nancy.

Also, for many sound reasons, authorities and investigative agencies often hold back information from public disclosure. For example, early on, Find Me's Dan Baldwin had dowsed some information that to him was nonsense. He was about to "shelve" it when fellow member Jacquelyn Kranz encouraged him to meet with the local police assigned to the case.

Some time later, the message came: "Tell Dan he connected some major dots for us."

To this day, Dan doesn't know what those dots were, just that they were important.

If you decide to become a channeler, begin by trusting the process, trusting your guides and trusting yourself. Allow what needs to come through to come through. Don't be surprised or upset if "you" begin speaking in a voice, dialect or even a language not your own. The information is important. Allow it to flow without filtering. There is always time later for analysis, commentary and further questions. Don't be alarmed at a change in body language or activity. You may experience some involuntary twitching in your arms and legs as your body adjusts to the higher vibrations.

The authors of *Opening to Channel* explain that, "As you channel, opening up to a higher vibration, you begin to change the molecular and cellular structure of your body, you literally bring more light into your cells."

When you begin your own channeling efforts, note any changes you experience so that you'll recognize the process as it unfolds and won't fear such changes or allow them to distract you from the task at hand.

Nancy's process

Nancy has been channeling for so long that she really doesn't have or need a formal process to do the work. She's so experienced at it that she can begin within seconds. For this book, she outlined a process beginning channelers can follow. Here are the basic steps.

Find a quiet time and place where you will not be disturbed. Close your eyes. Say a prayer.

For example, Nancy asks her guides, teachers and loved ones to come in and to deliver information that's for the highest and greatest good for all.

Visualize each chakra (see Chapter Seven). See the color associated with each one and activate them one at a time from bottom to top. Visualize a beam of white light running from bottom to top, connecting with the light of heaven.

Once the chakras are activated, visualize your Third Eye opening up. Nancy actually "sees" the eyelid pulling up and a beam of light shooting out to see the truth.

Allow the information to be delivered by whatever means it comes in. You may see, hear, feel, smell or think valuable information.

"I believe it's very important to study meditation and visualization. These are key tools, and you need to know how to use them properly," says Nancy.

She emphasizes the need to practice your skills. Once you start channeling, avoid the temptation to edit or filter the information. Something that doesn't make a bit of sense to you may make perfectly good sense to an investigator or to search and rescue personnel.

"Don't try to analyze or use logical thinking. Just deliver all the information you get. Allow the right side of your brain to take charge," Nancy states.

"Open your heart and trust the process, your guides and yourself.

Channeling will give you the wise teacher you seek, one who comes from within rather than without.

Orin and Daben, Beings of Light

Forensic Astrology

with Dave Campbell

> *Ride the tributaries to the sea.*
> *~ Arabian Proverb*

If one defines "the sea" as a great body of information about missing people, then there are many tributaries, pathways, leading to that destination. As we've seen, the members of Find Me follow many different paths. Tarot cards, channeling, pendulum dowsing, dreaming and other techniques are employed.

Astrology is one of those tributaries. Astrology is defined as the "doctrine of the stars," a science holding that the sun, moon, planets, stars and other heavenly bodies influence human activity. Dave Campbell applies the techniques of astrology to the search for missing persons, and therefore has become an authority on the subject of "forensic astrology."

Dave's story

Dave has always been interested in the metaphysical side of life. He's always been able to sense things about people. He's also been able to sense the spirits that are around. These sensations began at an early age.

On one occasion, when in the home of a friend of his mother, Dave began to feel very strange. He felt a presence and could see "faces." There were several rooms that he just wouldn't enter because a very palpable fear held him back at the doorway.

Dave asked his mother about the strange occurrences, wondering if there were such things as ghosts. She told him about "poltergeists," a German word for "noisy spirits" that sometimes wreak havoc in homes. Years later, Dave spoke with his mother's friend about the encounters, and the woman confirmed that paranormal activity occurred in the rooms he had feared to enter.

ESP actually helped improve Dave's report card. When he was in the third grade, his teacher noted that he wasn't paying attention in class. His mother enrolled him in a course called Alpha Dynamics, a discipline about using the alpha state to program the subconscious mind. The techniques helped improve memory, attention, energy, self healing and psychic ability
.

One of the key factors in developing his psychic abilities was a mother who encouraged such development.

"She would play psychic games with me and my two sisters, such as blindfolding us, then putting objects in a box to see if we could 'sense' what was inside," says Dave.

He began studying the Tarot while in his teens and, by the time he was in his early twenties, Dave's interest in the psychic world was even stronger.

While attending the funeral of a young boy, the son of a former girlfriend, Dave had the unnerving experience of sensing the spirit of the child sitting next to him. He kept these sensations to himself.

"I couldn't say anything to anyone because they would think I was crazy," he says.

A short time later, Dave and a friend visited a professional psychic. As the woman began the reading, she said, "Did you have an old girlfriend whose son has just passed?"

Dave was stunned, and his friend was in tears. This validation of his abilities spurred him to begin a two-year program of study into the psychic world. He began to study astrology under the guidance of a professional astrologer. He became a clinical hypnotherapist and enrolled in the Astrological Institute, the first accredited school of astrology.

One of the instructors conducted an experiment in which the students were given a series of crimes to solve using only astrological methods. The instructor would give them charts of a victim and three or four suspects. She even brought in a district attorney to show how astrology could be a useful law enforcement tool. The students "blew him away" by providing clues known only to his office.

Later, Dave became a certified research medium at the University of Arizona with Dr. Gary Schwartz and is currently a Windbridge certified research medium (WCRM) with Dr. Julie Beischel. He is also a certified professional astrologer with the American Federation of Astrologers (PMAFA). He is the author of *Forensic Astrology: Solving Crimes with Astrology* published by the AFA.

He is the author of *Forensic Astrology: Solving Crimes with Astrology*, published by the American Federation of Astrologers.

Dave's method

Dave is a clairvoyant, clairsentient and clairaudient.

"When working on the case of a missing person, I go into a meditation asking for information about the person, where he or she is, what happened, and any other information that would help with the case," he says. "I start receiving impressions, scenes, words, names and feelings. If the person has passed away, sometimes he or she actually comes to me during the meditation, often providing information and messages."

Dave writes down all these impressions.

His specialty is forensic astrology.

"Astrology uses the sun, moon, the planets, the signs of the Zodiac belt, the exact placement of the planets, and the aspect they are making with each other. The information necessary is the individual's date of birth, time of birth and place of birth."

Dave also uses asteroids in his analysis, as they are also named after mythological persons, places and things. Astrology can give clues about what has happened, the motive for the crime, locations to investigate, whether the individual is alive or dead, and can eliminate or pinpoint suspects.

The branch of astrology Dave uses is called "horary astrology," which is erecting a chart when the question is asked of the astrologer.

"The belief is that when a question is asked, the universe (God) already has the answer. Erecting the astrology chart for that exact time is the answer the universe is providing. Horary is amazingly accurate and is part of my belief in 'synchronicity,'" what most people wrongly call coincidence.

When brought into a case, Dave erects a chart for the last time the individual was seen, including date, time and place. He also may erect a crime-scene chart with the same information. He compares these charts with the birth charts of the missing person or victim of crime. If the suspects are known, he also looks at their charts.

Dave employs a two-step process. First he erects the appropriate astrological charts, then he uses his psychic skills to get additional information.

"I first look at the birth chart to see if there's a natural tendency for violence, rape, kidnapping and so on. Then I check to see what was going on astrologically with the person on the day of the crime or disappearance to see if anything was triggered in their charts causing that person to act out their behaviors."

The final step is to compare the victim's chart against the perpetrator's chart. If the two charts line up with astrological connections, Dave adds the asteroids with the names of the people involved.

"If the names of the asteroids line up in the charts, this is the final determining factor as to who was responsible. If there's a direct match between victim and suspect, then the suspect is the one responsible for the crime. Astrology is like DNA: There are no coincidences."

Forensic astrology involves erecting a number of charts: the natal (birth) chart of the victim, the natal chart of the suspect(s), the event chart (day/time/event), and the horary chart.

These must be compared with each other to get a result.

Here's an example of how using asteroids in missing-person and criminal cases works. The asteroid Persephone or Prosepina is named after a goddess who, in ancient mythology, was abducted and taken to the underworld by Pluto. Often, there are strong connections between Persephone and the charts of abducted children, and there will be strong connections between the abductor and Pluto.

Toro is an asteroid connected with extreme violence and rage. It's prominent in the chart for O.J. Simpson. Asteroid Prosepina is prominent in the chart for Patty Hearst, a victim of one of the most prominent kidnapping cases in the latter half of the twentieth century.

To see clearly is poetry, prophecy, and religion – all in one.
-John Ruskin

Finding Your Own Find Me

with Kelly Snyder

> *A rock pile ceases to be a rock pile the moment a single man contemplates it, bearing within him the image of a cathedral.*
> *~ Antoine de Saint-Exupery*

Kelly Snyder is the man who saw the "cathedral" and decided to build a group of individuals dedicated to finding missing people and solving crimes. Find Me is the product of his vision. (See Chapter One for how

Find Me was formed.)

There are a few psychic-detecting organizations out there, and Kelly believes there should be more. Every state and every country should have at least one such group. He is actively involved in encouraging and supporting the formation of groups such as Find Me. His experiences in each field, law enforcement and working with psychic detecting, provides a unique perspective on the challenges and opportunities found in the most challenging and most rewarding endeavor.

Finding Fred

One of the most rewarding endeavors began with the arrival of an e-mail from Santa Fe, New Mexico, in Find Me member Dan Baldwin's mail box. It was a request to help a friend in Scottsdale, Arizona. Her boyfriend's brother, Fred, was missing. Perhaps Find Me would be interested in helping. Dan immediately contacted Kelly, who spread the word to the group.

Little was known about the disappearance. Although his brother was on a trip, Fred had been in daily contact. He rented movies, returned them, and used an ATM machine. When his brother called, he asked what time they'd be back from the trip, as if anticipating the return. Nothing seemed out of the ordinary. And then Fred just disappeared.

Clues from Find Me started coming in quickly. Some were vague. Fred was wandering the streets...near a building with an ATM...walking on pavement within sight of buildings...he will continue to wander....

Other information was more specific. A number of Find Me members noted that Fred's disappearance was caused by a failure to stay on his medication. Others got the impression that he had a "dual" personality or experienced serious mood swings.

As it turned out later, Fred was bi-polar and had "gone off his meds." Several members noted that he was not in physical danger. One e-mailed, "Spirit tells me 'He's fine. He's fine.'"

The information kept coming in, and some of it was quite specific. Fred is in California. He's in the San Francisco Bay Area. He's wandering the streets. He can be found in or near homeless shelters and soup kitchens. Kelly assembled the pieces of the puzzle and passed along the information to the appropriate authorities. He also provided the information to the family because sometimes it has more significance to a family member than to the police.

Part of the Find Me mission is to counsel families in such confusing and stressful times. Kelly, himself a retired law enforcement officer, often explains police procedures so families can understand and appreciate the process and how it works.

Armed with this information, Fred's brother headed to the Bay Area. In less than three months from receiving that original note from Santa Fe, Find Me received a much happier e-mail.

"Kelly: Just to let you know that (Fred's brother) found Fred in San Francisco last Saturday. We had sent out the information to everyone that we and Fred knew in the Bay Area and through that he was spotted by a former co-worker...the people he talked to said...if he was looking for a homeless person he might try the kitchen down the street that fed people. When (Fred's brother) got there, Fred was standing in line...and he came home to Scottsdale...thank you again for your assistance."

A message to law enforcement

Those in law enforcement, and search and rescue teams, should look upon psychic gifts as tools and nothing more, but certainly nothing less. People with these gifts should be allowed and encouraged to use them. The physical, mental and emotional well being, and in many cases the very lives of individuals are on the line. The authorities should welcome help and guidance from all reliable sources.

Find Me is a reliable source. As of this writing, the group has worked forty-eight cases and, so far, only three police departments have refused to accept information.

"In my opinion, this is the same as refusing to accept phone calls from concerned citizens who may have information relating to the case at hand," says Kelly.

Indeed, why should an anonymous tip from a source about whom the authorities have no information be given greater credence than the insights from a hard working group of people dedicated to and focused on solving the crime?

In those few instances in which help from Find Me was refused, the reasons given were weak. We don't believe in psychics. We have never heard of a case being solved by psychics. We are concerned about public opinion.

Someday, Kelly and the members of Find Me would love to change the mindset of "We." If you've never used a psychic, or met a psychic, or researched cases that psychics have worked on and solved, then how can you make those assessments?

"It makes zero sense to take a position like that without knowing anything about the process," he says.

It's advice to law enforcement from someone with more than a quarter-century's experience: Don't let ignorance, ego or lack of knowledge keep you from accepting potentially valuable information.

Fortunately, many authorities are more open to help, regardless of the source. While working with a retired New York City detective on a missing-

person case in Florida, Kelly was told, "I'll take information from the devil if I can find a missing child."

During another missing-person investigation, in Arizona, an FBI agent stated, "I have never solved an investigation on my own and can always use some help."

An Arizona police detective told a member of Find Me, "Off the record, my biggest case last year was solved by a psychic."

Doors and minds are opening. As previously noted, people and organizations are now seeking out Find Me.

"What law enforcement needs to comprehend is that we're not asking you to believe in this type of phenomenon. Just accept it for what it is. Accept the information and see if it parallels facts that you're already aware of in your investigation. Secondly, if your investigation is going nowhere, then look at the psychic information as potential new leads or clues that may help solve your investigation," says Kelly.

The frustration he sometimes feels is, for the most part, temporary. The response to Find Me's work from local, regional, state and federal authorities has been overwhelmingly positive. If there is a single, overriding complaint expressed by Kelly and the members of Find Me, it's the lack of feedback.

"I guess I can't expect a call every day with updates from the detectives, but I believe the tables will turn in our direction when our success ratio is higher."

The psychics doing this work are volunteering their time and talent. It's challenging for them to continue working their magic when they never receive feedback. They need that information to validate their work, to see if they've somehow headed off in a wrong direction, and to fine tune their efforts.

Here's an example of why feedback is essential.

A member of Find Me was seeking clues about the disappearance of a little girl in Texas. He received a considerable amount of verifiable detail, and filed a report. His information pointed to events, people and locations in and around Santa Fe, New Mexico. Sadly, every bit of information was wrong. Nothing at all tallied with the missing-girl case. He chalked it up to having a bad day, and he vowed to work harder and more clearly next time.

More than half a year later, he was visiting friends in Santa Fe when he noticed a missing-child poster taped to the door of a convenience store. The details of a boy's disappearance matched the information the psychic had filed regarding the missing girl from Texas. Later when he checked his copy of the report he discovered that the day the boy disappeared was the day he conducted the reading for the missing girl.

The world of the paranormal is a strange place. Somehow, the psychic "wires" had become crossed and the psychic had tapped into one case while reading another.

The point? Had he received feedback, he would have known that he was following the wrong path in looking for the girl. More than that, the amount of verifiable information received would have sparked his curiosity. He would have researched other cases to see if there was a match, and he could have passed on the information to the authorities looking for the boy.

If you're interested in forming or joining a group like Find Me, realize that your chances of getting feedback from the authorities are less than 2 percent. They just don't make the effort. The only way to keep track of what's going on is by following the story in the local media, by checking information on the Internet, and with family and friends.

That's an unacceptable situation, but for now you'll have to accept it. Those are, unfortunately, just the rules of the game. In fairness, it should be noted that police are not required to share information outside of law enforcement. Additionally, sharing some information may violate the rules of evidence or department policy.

"My point is that you should not stop providing information through a group like ours or a group of your own," says Kelly. Don't sit on potentially valuable information, regardless of the reception you think you might receive. Lives could be at stake."

Expect to evolve

Expect evolution when forming and maintaining a psychic-detecting group. During the first year of Find Me's existence, lots of changes were made. We devised a form that outlines most of the information needed by law enforcement agencies. It categorized information in such a way that it was easier for Kelly to extract, formalize and send on to the appropriate investigative body. It even incorporates a section at the end for narratives to explain the categories in greater detail or to provide additional material. The form is considered a work in progress and will probably be continually improved and adapted to the challenges ahead.

Criteria for acceptance in Find Me

Anyone seeking membership in Find Me will be interviewed about their abilities and success level, and complete biographical and contact information will be needed. Each new member must understand that the group operates as volunteers and that there is no cost for services. Each member must agree to those terms, and to abide by the rules and guidelines of the organization.

"This is not an association for glory hounds or treasure seekers," says Kelly. Find Me seeks neither fame nor fortune, and the reasons for its involvement in a case are purely honorable.

"Starting a group similar to ours is easy, and I'm more than willing to assist anyone who may want to get involved. Everything we have can be shared and, needless to say, there are more missing children and unsolved investigations than one group can handle," says Kelly.

Ideally, such groups will eventually be located in every state and every country.

Working with police and other agencies

Anyone forming or joining a group such as Find Me will be working with police and other agencies. It's essential that you understand how these agencies function so you can augment, rather than hamper, their work.

Most police departments have the best intentions when they accept or are assigned to an investigation. How well they carry out that investigation depends on a wide range of factors: personal experience, individual commitment, size of the force, amount of training, street knowledge, gut instinct, specialty training, financial and other resources, and case load. Each factor can have a dramatic effect on any given case.

Most police departments pair an experienced senior officer with a junior officer so that the "rookie" can benefit from the knowledge and experience of the older and (hopefully) wiser officer. As a volunteer investigator, you may be working with an experienced pro who's been around or a rookie right out of the academy. You'll probably be working with both.

Be aware that some departments overload their officers, which creates a backlog. Often, a lot of time passes without much really being accomplished. Another chief reason for delays in an investigation often rests with the forensic lab. They usually run six to twelve weeks behind on lab reports and processing. Realize that the professional investigators assigned to the case may be just as "antsy" as you are to solve the case, but they may be hamstrung by factors outside their control.

The loyalty of Find Me members is directed to law enforcement because most everyone in those agencies is there for the right reasons. You'll periodically encounter exceptions. Some professional investigators drag their feet, some are incompetent, and others won't hesitate to lie to you. As a volunteer, it's imperative that you adopt a professional attitude and demeanor. Look at every situation and act according to the long-term view. Despite the shortcomings of any given officer or investigator, you'll want to maintain a strong relationship with the department.

Think in terms of achieving the greatest good over the longest period of time. The fact is, if they're listening to you and accepting your information, you're well ahead of the game.

To cite one example of how it works, there was a case in Oaklawn, Illinois, near Chicago. Kelly received a desperate e-mail from the mother of Eric, who had been missing for roughly five months. The mother, whom we'll call Pam, stated that she wasn't getting much help from the police. Specifically, she didn't get a warm and fuzzy feeling about the way the detectives were handling the case.

"I accepted the case, but also stated that we work with police and not just families. Our information could possibly name an exact suspect, and we don't want the families becoming vigilantes," Kelly recalls.

"The detectives wouldn't return my phone calls, so I asked Pam to make an appointment with the chief or assistant chief of the department, but not to let them hand her off to any other department authority. I gave her a list of questions to ask the chief, and advice on how to respond to questions and comments I was certain he would ask of her."

Pam met with the chief shortly thereafter, and the result was better than Kelly expected. The chief took the two detectives off the case, and he assigned two new detectives.

"What really surprised me was that when Pam told the chief about our group, he stated that he wanted to speak with me and deal with me personally. Almost immediately, Chief Bill Villanova and I were on the phone, and I was sharing psychic information with him about what the group had provided to me. He was honest in telling me he had no experience working with psychics, but was more than willing to 'give it a shot' in order to solve the investigation. He further stated that I was to give him a call periodically, and he would share with me the progress on the investigation," Kelly remembers.

"This is what I mean when I say that the police are willing to do whatever they can to help families, but are sometimes unable or unwilling to work with psychics because of their lack of knowledge about the issue. Having someone in law enforcement as a buffer to the police on behalf of the family is the best way to go in these matters, especially when dealing with psychics."

Kelly offers another example of why police don't like dealing with psychics. Imagine a high-profile case. Instantly, the department starts getting twenty or thirty phone calls a day from psychics, along with witnesses, concerned citizens and others. Large departments can handle most of the telephone traffic, but small departments get frustrated with the calls, especially if they have little or no knowledge about psychics.

Almost every psychic who has had the nerve to make that phone call to the police usually gets a less than positive response, so this is why it's so hard for psychics to get involved.

"The world needs more groups like Find Me, so that more and more police departments can use this extremely powerful tool!" Kelly emphasizes.

Accepting cases

The process of engaging Find Me is simple. A member gets a call from a friend, a family member, someone in law enforcement or search and rescue. Our website has also provided an investigatory gateway to the group.

The information is funneled to Kelly, who distributes it to the entire group. Those who can work on the case "do their thing," then file reports with Kelly. All members are required to file a report within fourteen days, even if the member has come up with nothing. This way, any information that comes in can be provided quickly to the appropriate authorities.

If the need for information is urgent, such as during an Amber Alert, the request for reports is so flagged. The data are consolidated and passed on to the appropriate investigative agency. Kelly also maintains contact with that authority during the investigation.

Centralization is important. The authorities, many of them highly skeptical of psychics, need to hear one, clear and steady voice, preferably someone with law enforcement or search and rescue experience who can "talk the talk."

If you're the organizer of your group, don't get discouraged. The response from your members will range from immediate and enthusiastic to practically non-existent. Some people will join for the highest motives. Others will hop onboard for a hoped-for free ride to fame and reward. They will drop off your membership roll rather quickly.

You will encounter skeptical authorities, and it's possible you'll occasionally face outright hostility. It's important to remember the reason you formed the group in the first place. The good you will accomplish will far outweigh the hassles you face along the way.

Understanding the process

"This topic would take twelve years, six months, two weeks, eleven hours and forty-three minutes to explain, and we'd still need more time for explanation. So I'll give you the short version," Kelly quips.

"Psychic detecting and the use of psychic abilities is not an exact science. As a matter of fact, I don't think it's in the realm of science."

Why the universe, God, the Goddess, Gaia, guides, spirits or whoever and whatever is out there don't provide complete answers is a mystery. It seems that, despite the skill of the individual or the collective abilities of the group, getting a complete picture of a case from start to finish just doesn't happen. One would think that if information was being sent in, it would be direct, obvious and complete instead of pieces of a puzzle. Why does the system, whatever that system may be, work this way? Why can't we ever get the full picture all at once? Why do we have to struggle to acquire and then make sense of fragments?

"I've asked those questions of psychics 'til my head hurts," says Kelly. The only sound answer is always the same. "That's just the way it is." And until that situation changes, psychic detectives will have to work according to the existing rules of the game.

Well, you now know the rules before you sign on.

"This process for now is the only one we have, but if we find one missing child or solve a senseless murder, then it makes sense to continue for that reason alone," says Kelly.

He works on the assumption that, someday, mankind will understand the answers to why psychic work is often so challenging, and that people will be able to perfect the system and solve crimes faster and easier.

"That's what motivates me to continue, and until I'm shown another way, that's exactly what I'll do."

Let the police do the policing
Psychic detectives who receive information about a case that's nearby

have a natural desire to get into the field and conduct some hands-on investigating. Many times, they'll do so without permission from, or even contact with, the investigating authority.

That attitude is misguided. Worse, it's dangerous. First, you are potentially putting yourself in harm's way. Some of the people or groups you will be investigating are dangerous, and some will be killers. Psychic detecting isn't a video game. It's for real.

The other significant danger is that your efforts will contaminate the crime scene. You could easily destroy evidence, alert a criminal that the authorities are closing in, or even jeopardize the outcome of the case. Provide your information directly to the police. If they don't take your information, explain that you'd like to proceed with your own investigation.

"That will get their attention," says Kelly.

He advises that you also seek the help of a local retired police officer or even the help of a private detective. The prosecutor's office in that jurisdiction is also another avenue.

If the information you're getting is strong, and you really are confident of its accuracy, then don't give up on the authorities. Be persistent.

"They are your best source and most, but not all, will try to do the right thing if you're convincing enough," says Kelly. Most departments have a public information officer to handle incoming information when detectives are covered up. You can certainly try that area.

As a last resort, you can approach the command staff. That would include the chief, assistant chief, commander, captain, lieutenant and sergeant. Remember, although they are public servants, these are very busy people, facing a lot of challenges. Always maintain a professional attitude and show proper respect.

You can also contact Find Me or any similar group that may be in your area. Some departments just don't want information from psychics because the investigators are non-believers or are afraid of criticism or who-knows-what.

As the coordinator at Find Me, Kelly knows how to get information into the right hands. Those hands may belong to the county sheriff, a prosecutor, another police department with parallel jurisdiction, or even a private investigator who knows the police in that particular area.

"I will make sure the information gets to someone in authority who will act on it. Believe me, someone will get the information," says Kelly.

A word on search dogs

As a leader or even a member of a group such as Find Me, you might be called upon to conduct, support or at least observe field work. Some of that work could involve search and rescue and cadaver dogs. These groups, located in just about every state, are for the most part staffed by volunteers. Their goal is simply to help law enforcement, search and rescue teams, and families find missing persons. The best search and rescue groups are those that are the best trained and those that have the best reputation.

"I'm sure that anyone who devotes his or her time to this has pure intentions, but it's always a good idea to identify who the best teams are in your area. Always rely on what the police have identified as the most reliable groups."

The most critical qualifications for search and rescue (SAR) teams are training and certification.

Certification is available from a number of sources, but real certification can come only from qualified instructors. Some groups will tell you that their animals are certified, but how they are certified is critical. They must meet the most stringent standards. The Find Me group works closely with SAR and cadaver dogs, and they are integral members of our team. This is the ideal situation.

Our partner is AZ-STAR (Arizona Search, Track and Rescue). Our canine response team (and it's a team in every aspect of the word) works with their dogs on a daily basis and continues the training process for both dog and handler. If you want to obtain SAR membership or view proper procedures for training and certification, you may contact us at our website at www.findme2.com or visit http://www.azstar.org.

We believe that it's essential to work closely with law enforcement and SAR groups in accordance with the appropriate rules, regulations and laws governing the situation. Evidence procedure and protection of the crime scene is extremely important. We realize that our efforts could enhance or hinder a crime-scene investigation. Often, a search scene can turn into a crime scene what it becomes clear that an abduction or murder has taken place. We are constantly aware of our responsibility to enhance, rather than hinder, the search process.

It's Find Me's position that processing the evidence is the sole responsibility of the investigating authority. It's essential for you to realize that your responsibility is to preserve the crime scene so that the authorities in charge can properly and legally investigate it. Processing evidence is not our responsibility.

If your group locates a crime scene, it's imperative that you remain at the scene and that you protect the scene from contamination. Don't leave the area until the proper investigative officers arrives. Again, your responsibility is to protect the scene, not investigate it. Your good intentions may cause more problems than you foresee. Play by the rules!

Some groups request donations, and this is not automatically a "red flag." There are legitimate expenses involved in purchasing, training, maintaining and using search dogs. Verify through the police that they are a credible organization. As a matter of fact, the police should be the agency to contact a search and rescue or cadaver dog group.

The only time a group such as Find Me should make such contact is when the authorities refuse to do so or give permission for the group to conduct the search. If your group has access to SAR dogs, you can offer those services when in contact with the investigative authority. The team or teams in your area should be easy to locate by contacting the local police.

Help groups

Another quick search of the Internet will reveal a large number of foundations, organizations and missing children/adults groups. It can be a real challenge to determine which are best suited to help you and your group the most.

Kelly's experience is with the National Center for Missing and Exploited Children (NCMEC), the premiere agency for missing children and runaways.

"They are the best place to start, but I highly recommend that you consider other groups in your area that offer the same assistance. Which one most closely matches the goals of your group and can provide you with the most assistance and guidance? Many people and groups have done what you are doing or are about to do. It would be foolish to refuse to learn and be guided by that experience," Kelly says.

The NCMEC can at least get the ball in play and start it rolling for you.

"Don't rely completely on them because their follow-through, from my personal experience, is not always the best because, being the premiere group, they are overwhelmed with work and requests for assistance," Kelly explains. "But virtually everyone associated with NCMEC is there for the right reason."

Here's a list of websites that provide information and assistance about missing children and adults:

National Center for Missing and Exploited Children – http://www.ncmec.org

National Center for Missing Adults – http://www.missingadults.org

Child Seek Network – http://www.childseeknetwork.com

Child Watch of North America – http://www.childwatch.org

Child Protection Education of America – http://www.find-missing-children.org

Vanished Children Alliance – www.vca.org

Christin Lamb Foundation – http://www.clamb.org

Jacob Wetterling Foundation – http://www.jwf.org

Morgan Nick Foundation – http://www.morgannick.com

Amber Alert – http://www.amberalert911.org

A cathedral, a community, an organization, any worthwhile endeavor begins as the idea within the mind of a man or woman. Finding missing children, finding missing adults and solving crimes are worthy goals, a noble calling. If you feel called to this type of work, follow that dream. Focus on the image of all the good you can accomplish, and start building!

We make a living by what we get; we make a life by what we give.
-Winston Churchill

Epilogue

All has been given, as the mystics say. We have only to open our eyes
and hearts to become one with that which is.
~ Henry Miller

As this book was being prepared for publication, Find Me was asked to help locate a man missing from the Phoenix area.

Darrin was divorced, but he and ex-wife Kathryn had remained close to provide a stable lifestyle for their six and nine year-old boys. Two years after their divorce, things weren't going well for Darrin. He was facing a number of challenges, including the loss of a job. Depression and anxiety had become regular features of his life.

During the week of August 20, 2006, he began sending letters to friends and family. These letters spoke of his love and of the fact that he'd "always be with them." Clearly he was saying goodbye.

When Kathryn asked if he was planning to harm himself, Darrin would only say, "I'm going away."

On August 27th, a number of his friends, alarmed at not hearing from him for a few days, visited his home. Darrin was gone, and so was his camping equipment. He was an avid camper, and his four-wheel drive vehicle allowed him access to thousands of remote camping sites throughout Arizona. Their concern turned to alarm when they discovered that Darrin's .44 caliber pistol was also missing.

Kathryn feared the worst, and contacted the Phoenix Police immediately. Unfortunately, rules are rules, and they could do nothing for seventy-two hours, at which time Darrin could be officially declared missing. Until then, he could only be considered an adult who might be "getting away from it all."

Kathryn got in touch with Darrin's friends and family, hoping that their knowledge of his habits and favorite camping sites might lead to his whereabouts. They agreed, but everyone realized that the task would be the equivalent of looking for the proverbial needle in a haystack. To say that Arizona's back country is rugged and remote is to make a significant understatement.

So desperate was the situation that she considered consulting a psychic. Several phone calls led to Cheryl Booth, a former member of Find Me who had left the group to pursue her career. Cheryl knew this was an ideal case for Find Me.

Kelly received an urgent e-mail from Kathryn on August 31st. He called her immediately and, after a brief discussion, agreed to take on the case. Find Me was notified, and the case was classified "urgent," meaning that an immediate response was necessary.

It's the group's goal to locate missing people alive and to assist the proper authorities in bringing them back to their friends and loved ones. When dealing with cold cases, in which such an outcome is unlikely, the goal is to at least bring closure. In Darrin's case, the "clock was ticking." Indeed, it had been ticking for several days.

The task was daunting. The search area had to be defined as "much of northern Arizona," an area of hundreds of thousands of acres of mountainous, heavily forested terrain with an uncounted number of back roads, logging roads, and 4WD trails.

Not every member of the group can respond to every case. For example, some may be on vacation or dealing with a personal or family crisis. Others just might not "get" any psychic information about a particular case. This is why the concept of Find Me is so powerful. When some members are "off" others will surely be "on." Three were definitely "on" for Darrin.

Amanda Schell didn't get much information about Darrin's specific destination. She believed that he was deceased because of an accident in his vehicle. She thought that he had been traveling northeast of Payson, Arizona, on Highway 260. That might sound rather vague, but the information narrowed the potential search area from "northern Arizona" to a large, yet specific, part of the state. Amanda didn't know it, but Darrin had several favorite camp sites in that general area.

Gabby, a member from Australia, also believed Darrin had passed on. She too "got" that he was in an area near Payson.

This proves an interesting and significant point. Psychics don't have to be on site to access valuable information about a case. This allows Find Me to provide local help from worldwide psychic resources. Gabby also said that Darrin was on a knoll or a hill overlooking a lake. She further identified the area by stating there was reflector tape or red paint on trees or wood poles near the campsite. She also stated that Darrin had stopped and spoken to an elderly man at or near a trading post. He would be found about fifteen minutes from that store. on a narrow dirt road surrounded by pine trees.

Dan Baldwin used his pendulum for map dowsing to come up with a number of specific clues. He believed Darrin was severely injured and unable to help himself. Darrin could be found on the Mogollon Rim, a rugged part of the national forest northeast of Payson. He was near Bear Canyon Lake, south of Mule Crossing off Forest Road #89.

Dan didn't know it, but the Bear Canyon area was one of Darrin's favorite camping sites.

Find Me had narrowed the search area to a challenging, but workable location.

Kelly relayed the information to Kathryn. Although several of Darrin's friends had been searching for their missing buddy, they hadn't found him. The information from Find Me gave them hope. Kathryn's boyfriend, John, decided he'd try to follow the clues. He drove to Payson and headed northeast on Hwy. 260, where he came across a "trading post" run by an elderly man. This is on top of the Mogollon Rim.

John took Forest Road #89, near Bear Canyon Lake, and drove for about three or four miles. He encountered a man standing in the road, a landowner wondering what John was doing up there. He handed over Darrin's missing person poster and explained that he was looking for a friend.

The landowner said he was sorry to report that he'd found the missing person that very morning while checking his property. Some days earlier, Darrin had set up his camp, crawled inside his tent and committed suicide. The authorities had been contacted. They'd conducted their investigation, and Darrin's body had already been moved from the site.

Darrin's tent had been set up on a little knoll overlooking the man-made lake. It was completely surrounded by pine trees. Many were marked for cutting with red paint. A number of wooden posts in the area were striped with red reflector tape.

This is how the Find Me philosophy comes together. Many psychics provide many clues. Some of them may be general, and some may be specific, but they all add to the overall picture.

Sadly, Darrin's case had become a cold case by the time Find Me was brought in. Still, the group was able to provide family and friends with a sense of closure. In this case, as with many others, Find Me also provides concerned and often frightened people with the knowledge that they are not alone facing perhaps the greatest challenge in their lives.

People around the world, although total strangers, truly care about them and their loved ones. More than that, these people are using their varied skills, without a thought to reward or recognition, to find that missing individual.

And where is Find Me today?

We're in the United States, Great Britain, Australia, Canada, France and Italy. We're working nine-to-five jobs, giving readings, teaching courses, babysitting kids or grandkids, taking care of ailments, going to church, working in civic clubs and service organizations, baking lasagna, hiking in the desert, and so on.

And, right now, some of us are throwing Angel cards, spinning pendulums, dreaming, meditating, creating star charts, remote viewing, seeing, hearing, feeling and listening to spirit guides and angels. Members are investing their time, their energy and their hearts trying as best they can to answer that desperate plea: "Find me.

Appendix

Missing Person/Homicide Form

CASE IDENTIFIER:

PERSON REPORTING:

DATE AND TIME:

STATUS OF MISSING PERSON: ALIVE – DECEASED – UNKNOWN

MISSING PERSONS LOCATION:

ADDRESS OR ROAD

TOWN OR CITY

COUNTY

STATE

COUNTRY

LANDSCAPE AND AREA DESCRIPTION

OTHER

SUSPECT PERSONAL AND PHYSICAL DESCRIPTION:

NUMBER OF SUSPECTS

NAMES

GENDER

RACE

AGE
WEIGHT AND BODY TYPE

HEIGHT

HAIR COLOR – STYLE – SIGNIFICANT CHARACTERISTICS

ADDITIONAL IDENTIFYING FEATURES

SUSPECT LOCATION:

ADDRESS OR ROAD

TOWN OR CITY

COUNTY

STATE

COUNTRY

LANDSCAPE AND AREA DESCRIPTION

OTHER

SUSPECT VEHICLE INFORMATION:

STYLE AND TYPE

MAKE

MODEL

COLOR

LICENSE PLATE NUMBER

ADDITIONAL IDENTIFYING FEATURES

COMMENTS – NARRATIVE – EXPLANATIONS FOR ALL LISTED CATEGORIES.

If you would like to learn more about Find Me or contact individual members, our official website is http://www.findme2.com/

Contributors

Dan Baldwin

Dan's psychic friends get a laugh when they first see his business card, which reads "Ghost." As a full-time freelance writer, he has co-authored or ghost-written more than forty books and CD programs on subjects ranging from real estate, management, sales and motivation, parenting, professional sports and psychic phenomena. Dan is the author of the *Caldera* series of Western novels. He has also won local, regional and national awards for his writing and film/video directing. These include a 2nd place in the Chicago International Film and Video Festival, a 1st place in the Mardi Gras Film and Video Festival, a national "Telly" award for television commercial writing/directing, and the American Chamber of Commerce Award of Excellence for film/video production.

Dan enjoys hiking and camping, especially in the "Lost Dutchman Mine" country of Arizona's Superstition Mountains. Dan also plays the Native American flute, is a certified clinical hypnotherapist specializing in past-life regressions, a Reiki Master, and he teaches a course called "The Practical Pendulum."

He is a student of the assassination of President John F. Kennedy and has lectured extensively at schools, colleges, civic organizations, and museums for many years.

Dan uses a multi-disciplinary approach to Find Me cases, but his primary tool is pendulum dowsing.

"I like the pendulum because there's no ambiguity. The answers are always yes/no, up/down, right/wrong and so on. It's a particularly effective technique for locating missing persons when used in conjunction with topographical maps," he says.

He often double-checks his pendulum readings with remote-viewing techniques, shamanic journeying or Tarot cards.

"I joined Find Me because the organization provided a door when I needed one. I had felt a strong call to find missing children for some time, and had been working cases on my own. Find Me provided a structure, co-workers, and a practical way to work directly with law enforcement and search and rescue groups around the world.

"Working with Find Me has been and continues to be one of the most challenging experiences in my life. It is also one of the most rewarding."

Dave Campbell, PhD

Dave Campbell, a full-time psychic medium and forensic astrologer, is the author of *Forensic Astrology: Solving Crimes with Astrology*. He is the owner of The Astrology Store, a metaphysical bookstore in Glendale, Arizona. Dave has been interviewed and has done readings on a number of Phoenix television and radio stations.

He is a clairvoyant, clairsentient and clairaudient who uses a number of methods for receiving information on missing-person cases, including the ability to communicate directly with those who have passed on. He defines forensic astrology as the practice of using astrology to solve crimes, profile suspects, eliminate or pinpoint suspects, assist in locating missing persons, resolve unsolved mysteries, determine motives, and give closure to families.

"I utilize all my skills when I work on a case: psychic, medium, astrology, to get information that can assist in finding a missing person. I have been doing professional readings for clients for more than ten years," he says.

"I joined Find Me because I was already doing this work on my own. A friend hooked me up with the group, and it was a perfect fit, as this is what I was looking for.

Stephen D. Earhart

Stephen is a practicing psychic medium with more than twenty years experience. He was born and raised in Dayton, Ohio, where he began showing psychic abilities at a very early age. He could meet someone for the first time and yet immediately know the past, present and even the future of that person.

He believes her psychic skills are a gift from God and are to be used to help other people. He moved to Bradenton, Florida, when his dad retired from government service. After finishing her schooling, he became a substitute teacher and youth worker. He served in those capacities for twenty-one years.

"My religion is spiritualist Christian, and I have read for many organizations and psychic fairs. I love people, young and old, and it gives me a sense of fulfillment to help others with these readings. As always, I like to say 'always keep the faith' throughout your life because God has a plan," Stephen says.

"I joined Find Me because of the quality of the project and for the people we help."

Mary Elizabeth

Mary is a Colorado native who was raised in Ohio. She returned home in 1990 and now resides in the beautiful mountains of Colorado. She is a child-protection caseworker and the mother of three children. Her contributions to Find Me, and her additional clairvoyant and personal healing work, are strictly not-for-profit.

Her skills include telepathy, clairaudience, clairsentience and channeling. Her specialties are remote viewing, high-sense perception, healing with internal viewing, and trauma memory recovery and healing.

"I joined *Find Me* purely by accident. I was working on a cold case here in Colorado when I began searching for other psychics to assist me. Catherine Kenney, a gifted astrologer, teacher, and a former member of our group, referred me to Kelly Snyder. As Kelly and I were talking, 'flashes' of a scene appeared. Apparently, it was a case Kelly and the group were working on. Needless to say, he was curious about my abilities, and I was equally curious about his group. The rest is history. I found Kelly, and the group found me. Did I say 'accident'?" she comments.

"My belief is that if you are truly here to help others, those in search of physical, spiritual and emotional healing will find their way to you. Similarly, these people are the ones who advance our intuitive abilities, and the tables are often turned as to who is healing whom. Toward that end, we naturally gravitate toward the things that will help us develop spiritually and psychically, regardless of our place in the psychic chain.

"In other words, if you seek, you will not only find, you will be found by like-minded individuals."

Jeanette Healey

"Since I was a young child, I have been walking 'a black and difficult path.' Most people would shy away from this, but there is a strength within, enabling me to cope," says Jeanette.

She became aware of her psychic ability at the age of five, when a lot of strange things began happening around her. She was seeing and hearing things that other people did not. Of course, people said that she just had a vivid imagination. Her paternal grandmother, a medium, explained the things that were causing her to be upset.

"To be told it was not my imagination, and that I was seeing spirits and entities for real, was a huge thing to rest on such small shoulders."

Jeanette has two grandchildren who are showing signs of psychic ability. She has not explained the psychic world to them in the same way.

"When you hear somebody calling 'Jeanette,' you turn, and nobody familiar is there; that can be upsetting and alarming. As an adult, I'm used to feeling foolish, smiling or saying 'hello,' and sometimes receiving strange looks from passers by," she says.

The "black path" Jeanette says she was and is on refers to the fact that, through her psychic abilities, she is shown murder victims, children and women who were in the public eye, including news and television. Why does this happen, she wonders.

Perhaps Spirit wanted her to help find the suspects or their bodies. She has also had dream and day visions related to national criminal information. Jeanette has worked with and for the police at different times over the years. She says it can be thrilling, but there is also a downside, which includes feelings of frustration and emptiness.

"The outcome can leave you with a sense of letting people down if you are only given small parts of the story. To do this work, you have to pick yourself up and say 'Thank God for this gift.'"

Jeanette came to Find Me by asking Spirit for someone with contacts who could help her help more people. She made some enquiries and was given a number for Chris Robinson, a member of the group. Although they did not meet face-to-face for five years, they discovered they shared a unique gift and were able to work cases together by phone. One day early in 2003, Chris told her about a small group of psychics in America who were freely giving their time helping people find missing loved ones. She contacted Kelly and became a member of the Find Me team.

"I joined Find Me because sharing one's gift with others is something special, which is why we have it," she says.

Sunny Dawn Johnston

Sunny Dawn Johnston is recognized as a loving and caring spiritual teacher who has helped thousands of people across the country find their own inner truth. As a child, with the support of her metaphysical parents, she was given the opportunity to find her own truth, beliefs and life path. She was a gifted child, and has since devoted her life to the enhancement of her natural gifts and to the application of these skills in helping humanity. Sunny has become nationally known and respected as an intuitive, medium and spiritual teacher.

She began volunteering as a psychic investigator for Find Me after sharing many of her experiences as a medium with a colleague and member of the group. Sunny shared how frustrated she was when she received messages from the spirit world through her readings and everyday life, but had no one to contact who would listen. She would have unexplainable information about murders and crimes, but had nowhere to go with the information and no way of helping solve the crimes.

As divine timing would have it, she was told about a group of people working together with that exact intent. Her colleague suggested she contact the group. Sunny has been a member of Find Me ever since.

Sunny is a certified spiritual counselor, Reiki master/teacher, ordained minister, hypnotherapist and certified medium. Sunny is also very passionate about her work as a regional Alzheimer's advocate and as a hospice volunteer with Dannion Brinkley's Compassion in Action Twilight Brigade.

As a national speaker, Sunny's dynamic methods effectively reach out to help people help themselves, which then gives them the tools to help others. Sunny has studied with many world-renowned speakers, teachers and healers, such as Dr. Doreen Virtue, Dr. Sonia Choquette, Louise Hay, Dr. Wayne Dyer and James Van Praagh.

She is actively involved in the spiritual community. Her classes at Maricopa County Community Colleges, Borders Books, city libraries and her own Healing Center are well-attended and very well-received.

In December 2003, Sunny founded Sunlight Alliance, a teaching and healing center in Glendale, Arizona. She felt there needed to be a place where people could go for guidance and support as they walk their own spiritual path. Sunlight Alliance offers classes designed to improve people's intuitive skills and knowledge about themselves as well as a variety of spiritual subjects.

Sunny has created several meditation CDs to help support people on their journeys of self discovery, spiritual awareness and healing.

Nancy Marlowe

Nancy Marlowe is a professional medium born with the gifts of clairvoyance, clairaudience, claircognizance, clairsentience, clairgustance (clear smell), remote viewing, mental telepathy, prophecy and healing. She is also an authentic channel for information.

As a medium, angels, dead people, guides and other entities communicate with her. She sees them, hears them and feels them. They show her what she wants to know. Nancy enjoys helping bring comfort to people who have lost loved ones by connecting to those on the other side.

When invited to join Find Me, she readily accepted. Nancy felt she could contribute by helping find missing people. It's her way of "giving back."

Nancy was severely injured in a car crash in 1997. Her doctors thought her outlook for recovery was grim. In fact, they thought she should have died. They don't understand why she lived. They don't understand how she is completely well. Nancy believes her faith in the unknown to heal brought about her total recovery. Today, she shares her gifts and knowledge with others…seeking to empower them also.

Nancy is a *magna cum laude* graduate who combines her teaching skills with her psychic gifts to teach others how to connect with their own intuition and their soul. She is an educator, speaker, author and consultant.

Joanne Miller

Joanne believes that when we understand the nature of our abilities, we need an avenue to pursue them, and we must also find the vehicle to deliver these gifts. In her case, finding Find Me required much trial and error, and many mental arguments. Finding the right place was a long and difficult process, but she knew that at the right time the right group of psychics would be found.

As is always the case in the universe, everything arrives on time, without delay, exactly when it should happen. The universe created the proper conditions to meet the person who would introduce her to this group. She also discovered that what she had thought were sidetracks were in reality, the course of study that prepared her to be in the same place as the other members of Find Me.

"I joined Find Me because it was time and I was ready," Joanne says.

Eileen Nelson

For more than thirteen years, Eileen has been working voluntarily as a psychic detective on missing persons and murder cases.

"It's been an honor to be with Find Me for the last two years, working *pro-bono*, alongside some very gifted people who truly care, to help solve these difficult cases and also offer closure to the grieving loved ones of those missing or murdered," she says.

Eileen is free to dedicate herself full time to this unusual, yet enlightening and fulfilling, work. Over the years, she has met some wonderful people and has been saddened to see the emotional pain that these types of crimes bring to the survivors of the victims of homicide or missing persons.

"If there is anything I can do to bring peace and closure to these families, then I am content to say I'm doing this job well. Though I can't say I've solved any cases, I have offered clues that have helped move the case along in a positive direction."

It's interesting how Eileen came upon Find Me. Jeanette Healey, another member of the group and now a good friend, had contacted her by email from England. She was amazed that someone from all the way across the world found her website. They chatted and compared notes, and Jeanette asked if she worked for an agency. Eileen was surprised by the question, as she worked alone at her home. Jeanette said that she had helped law enforcement agencies in the U.K. with her intuitive abilities. Eileen found that idea appealing, but continued working alone.

It wasn't long after, however, that she began to volunteer with Find Me, introduced by Joanne Miller, a mutual friend on the team at the time. She was delighted to be in a group represented by Kelly Snyder, who has a great deal of law enforcement experience.

"This is the reason I joined Find Me. I wanted that connection to experienced law enforcement, and Find Me is the perfect team for that to happen. We are all committed to not only offering insights and clues, passed onto law enforcement, but we are able to offer peace and comfort to the families of those missing and murdered. With growing awareness of our efforts over time, we can hope to reach more and more law enforcement agencies willing to work with professional intuitives, coordinating our efforts to a common goal. I'm so glad I found Find Me!"

Loretta Greazzo

Loretta was born and raised in Brooklyn, New York, by Italian Catholic parents. Although she had six sisters, and the house was never empty, she always had an uneasy feeling because she felt surrounded by people who were not physically there. It was very frightening to grow up with this ability, Loretta recalls. She never had someone to talk to about her fears because she didn't want anyone to be laughed at, and she didn't want people to think she was crazy. She kept her abilities to herself.

Loretta's friends thought she was "a little strange" because she knew things before they happened.

"Growing up, I always felt a little different from my peers. Never better, just different, and I could never pinpoint it. At times, I felt I just didn't fit in. What I did know growing up was that I needed to help people," she says.

Her psychic and mediumistic abilities got stronger and stronger as she grew. She started having visions.

"More information psychically was flowing through me, and I started to really pay attention to the feelings I was getting of just knowing what was going to come to pass. I was realizing there was a lot more to what was going on with me, and that what I was feeling and sensing was not just common sense but something more powerful."

Loretta started reading up on the subject, and she started looking for any classes relating to the metaphysical and paranormal world. After about a year, she realized that what she had been doing all her life was truly a blessed gift. She then started getting messages from deceased people, who seemed to come during her meditations.

She started offering classes on "Developing Your Own Psychic and Medium Abilities" at various locations in the Phoenix area.

"We all have these abilities, some stronger than others, but if you have the desire, you can bring out the abilities in you. I knew now I could help people by giving them closure in letting them know that their deceased loved ones are fine," she says.

Her quest was to find out how to reach the people who needed and wanted help with either connecting with their deceased loves ones for peace and closure, or those who just wanted some psychic information and help.

"I met someone through a friend who was involved with Find Me. I spoke to Kelly Snyder at length. After hearing what he had to say, and seeing the good the group was doing, I decided to join. Find Me is a professional, dedicated, caring and compassionate group of people, and I am honored and blessed to be a member. I have finally found the path I was meant to be on to use the gifts I was blessed with, to help people in need."

Chris Robinson

Christopher was born in England. Until the age of thirty six, he reported having dreams two or three times a year, dreams that appeared to come true a few days later. The frequency of the prophetic dreams increased, and since October 1989, they have been an almost daily occurrence. He has co-written a book, *Dream Detective,* which was published in 1996 and again in
1997.
Chris came to the attention of London's New Scotland Yard in 1984, and has had regular contact with either police or intelligence officers from

British customs and criminal intelligence services ever since.

He has given public demonstrations on live national television, showing his ability to dream the contents of sealed containers. The main feature of his dreams: They show him what will occur in his life the next day. This, he says, is the case even if he could not possibly know what would happen. An example would be dreaming of a plane crash or some other completely unforeseeable event a day before it happens.

Chris joined Find Me in 2004 and has remained an active member. He has brought other psychics into the group, and has been instrumental in coordinating international efforts with Japan.

"I was there before Find Me was formed, so it was natural for me to join," he says.

Amanda Schell

Amanda was adopted at birth by a prominent Jewish family well known in the film industry, but was not told of her adoption until age thirty three.

She grew up in a loving household, and spent many years traveling with her adoptive father, mother and younger sister to various TV and movie sets throughout the U.S. and Europe. She was drawn to athletics, and became proficient in dance, tennis, aerobics, gymnastics and other sports. Amanda had an idyllic childhood that was filled with joy and boundless optimism.

At age thirty two, she sustained a serious injury to her neck that would eventually be the source of great spiritual advancement. The injury was characterized by unrelenting chronic pain. Having tried every conceivable treatment to help her condition, Amanda had no other choice but to undergo radical spinal neck surgery, which was unsuccessful.

After years of pain, and with no religious orientation or belief system to assist her, Amanda knelt and prayed for wellness and relief with the most soulful of prayers. Her extraordinary journey into spiritual awakening began. Suddenly she found herself completely bathed in an incomprehensible light of love and energy of divine origin. Her prayer was answered with a full-blown illumination experience from which she emerged with great joy, fulfillment and a sense of the unlimited nature of the human spirit.

The optimism she once felt as a child was restored, and she has discovered how to ignite the illumination experience on an almost daily basis.

An unexpected byproduct of this illumination experience has been her awakening of psychic sensitivity. Amanda was invited to join Find Me. She uses psychometry, meditation and clairvoyance as her primary methods in psychic casework.

"I became a member of 'Find Me' because I felt this special ability was given to me as a gift to assist others. Making a positive difference in the world by helping those in need brings me great joy. I truly feel grateful and honored to be a part of our "Find Me.""

Kelly Snyder

Kelly began his law enforcement career at the age of twenty five, when he joined the U.S. Customs Service. Later he transferred to the Drug Enforcement Administration, where he served for twenty-one years.

Since retirement, Kelly has applied his investigative skills as the director of security for Westin Hotels and Resorts, the regional manager of Safeco (Special Investigations Unit), instructor IED Protocols for the Department of Homeland Security (TSA), and as an investigator for the National Center for Missing and Exploited Children. He also joined Big Brothers Big Sisters in 2001. He founded Find Me in 2002.

"I created Find Me for two very basic reasons: one, to support the efforts of law enforcement and, two, to provide closure to families and individuals affected by the loss of a friend or member of the family," he says.

Find Me

Made in the USA
Charleston, SC
21 January 2013